The Right to Know: Epistemic Rights and Why We Need Them

We speak of the right to know with relative ease. You have the right to know the results of a medical test or to be informed about the collection and use of personal data. But what exactly is the right to know, and who should we trust to safeguard it?

This book provides the first comprehensive examination of the right to know and other *epistemic rights*: rights to goods such as information, knowledge and truth. These rights play a prominent role in our information-centric society and yet they often go unnoticed, disregarded and unprotected. As such, those who control what we know, or think we know, exert an influence on our lives that is often as dangerous as it is imperceptible

Beginning with a rigorous but accessible philosophical account of epistemic rights, Lani Watson examines the harms caused by epistemic rights violations, drawing on case studies across medical, political and legal contexts. She investigates who has the right to what information, who is responsible for the quality and circulation of information and what epistemic duties we have towards each other. This book is essential reading for philosophers, legal theorists and anyone concerned with the protection and promotion of information, knowledge and truth.

Lani Watson is Research Fellow at the University of Oxford, UK

Routledge Focus on Philosophy

Routledge Focus on Philosophy is an exciting and innovative new series, capturing and disseminating some of the best and most exciting new research in philosophy in short book form. Peer reviewed and at a maximum of fifty thousand words shorter than the typical research monograph, *Routledge Focus on Philosophy* titles are available in both ebook and print on demand format. Tackling big topics in a digestible format the series opens up important philosophical research for a wider audience, and as such is invaluable reading for the scholar, researcher and student seeking to keep their finger on the pulse of the discipline. The series also reflects the growing interdisciplinarity within philosophy and will be of interest to those in related disciplines across the humanities and social sciences.

Confucianism and the Philosophy of Well-Being
Richard Kim

Neurofunctional Prudence and Morality
A Philosophical Theory
Marcus Arvan

The Epistemology and Morality of Human Kinds
Marion Godman

A Defence of Nihilism
James Tartaglia and Tracy Llanera

The Right to Know
Epistemic Rights and Why We Need Them
Lani Watson

For more information about this series, please visit: www.routledge.com/Routledge-Focus-on-Philosophy/book-series/RFP

The Right to Know

Epistemic Rights and
Why We Need Them

Lani Watson

Routledge
Taylor & Francis Group

LONDON AND NEW YORK

First published 2021
by Routledge
2 Park Square, Milton Park, Abingdon, Oxon OX14 4RN

and by Routledge
605 Third Avenue, New York, NY 10017

First issued in paperback 2022

Routledge is an imprint of the Taylor & Francis Group, an informa business

Publisher's Note
The publisher has gone to great lengths to ensure the quality of this reprint but points out that some imperfections in the original copies may be apparent.

British Library Cataloguing-in-Publication Data
A catalogue record for this book is available from the British Library

Library of Congress Cataloging-in-Publication Data
A catalog record has been requested for this book

ISBN: 978-1-138-34379-5 (hbk)
ISBN: 978-1-032-03910-7 (pbk)
ISBN: 978-0-429-43891-2 (ebk)

DOI: 10.4324/9780429438912

Typeset in Times
by KnowledgeWorks Global Ltd.

Contents

Acknowledgements

I am incredibly grateful to the many people who have given their time and energy to help me write this book. From the intensity of broad-ranging, heated debates about the central concept, in the early stages (especially Wayne Riggs), to the all-important details of grammar and phrasing, in the final draft (especially Lynn Watson). Many have also provided questions and comments along the way. In particular, I would like to thank Claire Ashford, Kiah Ashford-Stow, Natalie Ashton, Jason Baehr, Dorit Bar-On, Heather Battaly, Cameron Boult, Quassim Cassam, Charlie Crerar, Michel Croce, Rowan Cruft, Carrie Figdor, Fani Gamon, Sanford Goldberg, Allan Hazlett, Ian James Kidd, Nathan Kellen, Maxime Lepoutre, Michael Lynch, Ian Macbeth, Euan MacDonald, Kay Mathieson, Aidan McGlynn, Adriana McNally, Daniella Meehan, Anthony Morgan, Maggie O'Brien, Robbie Porter, Lea Raible, Hazel Roberts, Mona Simion, Martin Smith, Nancy Snow, Dorrik Stow, Jay Stow, Alessandra Tanesini, Alice Theobald, Lynne Tirrell, Dennis Whitcomb, Helen Wilkinson and Jonathan Wilson. Lastly, the ideas and arguments in this book have benefited significantly from the insightful scrutiny of my wife, and muse, Lynn Tonner. I have benefited even more so from her confidence and support.

This book was written with the support of a Leverhulme Trust grant, no. R444. The opinions expressed are those of the author and do not reflect the views of the Leverhulme Trust.

Introduction

Don't forget that when we plan to enshrine freedom in any field, the first requisite is the right to know[1]

Knowing matters. What we know, or think we know, and what we don't know determines much of what we do. We decide what to buy, what to risk, who to trust, and who to vote for on the basis of what we know, or think we know, about the world around us. 'Knowledge is power' as Sir Francis Bacon's famous adage boldly states.[2] The other side of the coin is less pithy but no less significant: ignorance disempowers. It limits our ability to make the everyday decisions of our lives, as well as the decisions that change our lives in important ways. Moreover, as Socrates insisted, thinking that we know something that we don't is the worst of all worlds. Better to see the limits of our individual and collective knowledge than to be misled into false certainty. In all of these ways and more, knowing matters. Those who control what we know, or think we know, exert an influence on our lives that is often as dangerous as it is imperceptible.

This control is a feature of contemporary life that has come prominently to the fore in the twenty-first century; the information-centric world that we identify as the 'Information Age'. In this world, more information is available faster than ever before and is deployed in the service of those ends that have distinguished humanity throughout its

---

1 Kent Cooper's Address on the Methods of Insuring World-Wide Press Freedom. Available at: https://timesmachine.nytimes.com/timesmachine/1945/01/22/88184102.pdf [Accessed: 3 December 2019].
2 This aphorism is usually attributed to Sir Francis Bacon. The Latin phrase "ipsa scientia potestas est" ('knowledge itself is power' or 'knowledge is His power'), occurs towards the end of his essay 'Of Heresies' in the *Meditationes Sacrae* (1597). The exact phrase "scientia potentia est" ('knowledge is power') appears for the first time in Latin in the 1668 version of *Leviathan* by Thomas Hobbes, who was Bacon's secretary for a period as a young man.

history: adaptation, innovation, dominance power. The new technologies of the Information Age have reframed the pursuit of these ends, ushering in the so called 'post-truth' era. Now it is not knowledge, so much as controlling what is and is not known, that issues in power. The problems that we encounter in this 'brave new world' are not, in essence, new ones. However, the recent changes to our informational – our *epistemic* – landscape have happened at breakneck speed and it is not surprising that our public institutions, including our educational, legal, healthcare, media and governmental bodies, have struggled to keep pace. In many respects, we still lack the conceptual resources and the vocabulary to make sense of and articulate the Information Age. This includes many of the new and more widespread harms that have been made possible by its advent.

This book seeks to illuminate a concept lying at the heart of many of the most significant challenges that we face in the information-centric world in which we live: *epistemic rights*. Put simply, epistemic rights are rights concerning goods such as information, knowledge and truth. These rights play an increasingly prominent role in our lives and communities and yet they often go unnoticed, disregarded and unprotected. By illuminating this concept, I seek to do three things. Firstly, to draw attention to epistemic rights as a distinct and unified class of rights. Secondly, to demonstrate the ubiquity of epistemic rights and epistemic rights violations in contemporary life. Thirdly, to provide a vocabulary with which to articulate the harms caused by epistemic rights violations. Ultimately, by doing so, I aim to advance the case for thinking and talking about epistemic rights.

I do so, not without caution. The language of rights is a powerful language and one open to abuse. I take this seriously and am by no means exclusivist about rights-talk, which is just one, albeit significant, feature of our moral landscape. Nonetheless, I believe that the power of rights-talk is one of the most compelling reasons to adopt it, with due caution, in the epistemic domain. The language of rights affirms the inextricably political character of the epistemic. It does so in a way that captures the often highly political nature of the real world. In a world defined by information, the epistemic is increasingly both the grounds and the substance of our moral and political decision-making. Talk of epistemic rights reflects this.

This politicising is increasingly commonplace in contemporary epistemology. Seminal works of early feminist epistemologists, such as Harding (1986), Jaggar (1983, 1989) and Hill Collins (1986, 2000), have emerged into the mainstream in recent years. This has been accompanied by epistemological work on themes ranging across the political spectrum, from fake news and the rise of social media, to conspiracy theories and radicalisation, to epistemic oppression and injustice (Fuller, 1988, 2018; Mills, 1998; Goldman, 1999; Tanesini, 2004; Fricker, 2007; Dotson, 2011, 2014; Coady, 2012; Medina, 2013; Lynch, 2016; Goldberg, 2018; Cassam, 2019). The epistemic rights-talk advocated in this book aligns with and advances this notable and, in my view, essential politicising trend.

A common feature of this growing literature is the use of examples and case studies drawn from the real world (as opposed to constructed). Such examples ground the less tangible aspects of epistemic life – belief, knowledge, truth – in real world situations and lived experiences. In line with this, I make extensive use of examples and case studies throughout the book. These provide rich content for the discussion and demonstrate the value of articulating and analysing the real world through the lens of epistemic rights. Lens is an apt metaphor. Talk of epistemic rights focuses, magnifies and clarifies the epistemic dimension of real-world issues and events, particularly in domains that are not typically or primarily spoken about in epistemic terms.

As I write, in the midst of the global Covid-19 pandemic, it is easy to see the valuable focus that such a lens provides in relation to issues of immediate concern. Issues, for example, surrounding open access to information about the virus among the international research community, the suppression or mistreatment of information about the virus by governments and media outlets, the spread of false information about the origins and prevalence of the virus online, conspiracy theorising about the purpose, effects and legitimacy of a potential vaccine, and so on. Ultimately, the present crisis is one of life and death but the moral and political decision-making that is required in order to resolve it is intricately bound up with an array of epistemic factors, many of which can be constructively viewed through the lens of epistemic rights.

I will not, however, take the current crisis as a central case in the book. Both its immediacy and evolving complexity make it a challenging and potentially distracting subject matter for the analysis of epistemic rights. Nonetheless, the case studies I use are drawn from diverse domains of public and private life and traverse a wide range of societal and political issues. I will begin by introducing one of these case studies here, which features centrally throughout the book. Several others will be introduced in the remaining chapters. The central case study focuses on the production and marketing of the opioid-based painkiller OxyContin, by the pharmaceutical giant Purdue Pharma, in the context of the ongoing US opioid crises.

A central case: Purdue Pharma

In May 2007, Purdue Frederick Company Inc., an affiliate of Purdue Pharma, along with three of its top executives were ordered to pay fines totalling $634 million after pleading guilty to criminal charges of misbranding in relation to the opioid-based painkiller, OxyContin. Among other things, the company falsely claimed that OxyContin was less addictive than other opioids and less subject to abuse. The court ruling came at the end of an extensive investigation into the company's long history of aggressive marketing practices, which began in the 1970s under the stewardship of the controversial marketing tycoon, Arthur Sackler.

In a recent book-length exposé, *New York Times* journalist Barry Meier (2018) argues that Sackler "helped pioneer some of the most controversial and troubling practices in medicine" (p.52). These include all-expenses paid conferences designed to promote OxyContin and recruit medical professionals to Purdue's National Speaker Bureau (Van Zee, 2009; Orlowski and Wateska, 1992), as well as significant bonuses for doctors prescribing OxyContin (averaging $71,500 in 2001, for example). Purdue also collected information on doctors' prescribing habits, targeting the highest opioid prescribers with branded promotional gifts and materials (Van Zee, 2009). These activities, alongside others, amounted to an aggressive and, at the time, unprecedented marketing campaign designed to influence the prescribing habits of doctors and compel them to prescribe OxyContin.

In its aggressive marketing of OxyContin, Purdue made liberal use of fabricated information about the addictive properties of the painkiller and repeatedly issued false claims about the effectiveness of the drug, the likelihood of harmful withdrawal symptoms, and the potential for abuse through diversion.[3] Purdue armed its sizable salesforce with graphics, charts and information which downplayed the addictive properties of OxyContin and trained salespersons to respond to concerns by conveying the (false) message that the risk of addiction was "less than one percent" (Van Zee, 2009 p.223). As reported by Patrick Radden Keefe in the *New Yorker*:

> As late as 2003, the FDA [Food and Drug Administration] sent Purdue a warning letter about ads that "grossly overstate the

---

3 Diversion involves crushing the drug to release the more potent and addictive payload contained within it.

safety profile of OxyContin by not referring in the body of the advertisements to serious, potentially fatal risks".[4]

There is much to be concerned about in this case: the use of aggressive marketing techniques and incentivisation in the healthcare industry, the monopolisation of pharmaceuticals for profit and the overriding failure of governmental or industry bodies to hold companies such as Purdue Pharma to account. The purpose of detailing the case here, however, is to highlight the prominent theme of false and misleading information that runs throughout.

Through its aggressive marketing of OxyContin, Purdue Pharma controlled the extensive and systematic spread of false and misleading information throughout the US medical community for the purpose of profit. In the 2007 trial, its company executives were forced to admit that Purdue had marketed OxyContin "with the intent to defraud or mislead".[5] In a news release from the US Attorney's Office following the case, US Attorney John Brownlee is quoted:

> Even in the face of warnings from health care professionals, the media, and members of its own sales force that OxyContin was being widely abused and causing harm to our citizens, Purdue, under the leadership of its top executives, continued to push a fraudulent marketing campaign ... In the process, scores died as a result of OxyContin abuse and an even greater number of people became addicted to OxyContin; a drug that Purdue led many to believe was safer, less abusable, and less addictive than other pain medications on the market.[6]

The deliberate spread of false and misleading information is central to the Purdue Pharma case. It amounts, as I will argue, to a serious and harmful violation of epistemic rights. This includes the epistemic rights of many of the medical professionals targeted by Purdue and those of the patients that they serve. It is important, I believe, that we understand the nature of these rights and the harms that are caused by their violation. I will return to the Purdue Pharma case throughout the book. It is just one case, among many, that demonstrates the

---

4 https://www.newyorker.com/magazine/2017/10/30/the-family-that-built-an-empire-of-pain# [Accessed 26 Nov 2019].

5 https://www.newyorker.com/magazine/2017/10/30/the-family-that-built-an-empire-of-pain# [Accessed 26 Nov 2019].

6 https://www.health.mil/Reference-Center/Publications/2007/05/10/The-Purdue-Frederick-Company-Inc-and-Top-Executives-Plead-Guilty [Accessed 6 Feb 2020].

need for common conceptual and linguistic resources to articulate and address a distinct form of serious and harmful misconduct in the epistemic domain.

Indeed, if the case of Purdue Pharma were anomalous, perhaps the call for epistemic rights-talk would be less pressing. However, even within the context of the US opioid crisis, Purdue is not alone. The ongoing crisis has culminated in over 2000 lawsuits, against a dozen or so major pharmaceutical companies across the US. In the first of these, heard in Oklahoma in August 2019, the pharmaceutical giant Johnson & Johnson were ordered to pay $572 million. Although a landmark case, the fine was significantly less than the $17 billion that the state of Oklahoma calculated it would need to deal with the effects of the opioid crisis. Health Policy and Law professor, Abbe R. Gluck noted, "The critical finding is that Johnson & Johnson engaged in false, deceptive and misleading marketing".[7] As with Purdue Pharma, such marketing constitutes a serious and harmful violation of epistemic rights.

The nature of the task

The nature of the present task is both philosophical and political. Often discussions of rights distinguish between two central questions. First, what is a right – or what does it mean to have a right? Second, what rights do we have? The first question is analytical; it asks for an analysis of the concept of rights. The second question is broadly political; it asks for an examination of the rights that we have or should have and for a justification of our having them. However, as Andrei Marmor (1997) notes, "Few philosophers ... doubt that these two issues, the analytical and the political, are closely related and the answers to them interdependent" (p.1).

I will ask both of these questions with respect to epistemic rights. Chapter 1 will be chiefly concerned with the analytical task presented by the first question: what are epistemic rights? Some of the more technical ground will be covered in this chapter and in Chapter 2. This ground is necessary in order to provide a firm foundation for the broadly political task presented by the second question. As such, while this book is certainly cast in the fires of analytic epistemology, the terrain is necessarily political and its ends are both philosophical and political.

---

7 https://www.nytimes.com/2019/08/26/health/oklahoma-opioids-johnson-and-johnson.html [Accessed 28 Nov 2019].

The discussion will, I hope, raise at least as many questions as it answers. Questions about who has the right to what information, who is responsible for the quality and distribution of that information, and who, in our lives and communities, is controlling the information that we see and the information that we don't. Ultimately, these questions reflect many of the familiar concerns of life in the Information Age. Some of them, I believe, are urgent. The issues they raise have been examined before in different guises. My claim is not that these are new questions but that framing them in terms of epistemic rights will help us to identify connections between previously disparate issues and domains of life and offer a vocabulary with which to express common underlying concerns. These questions reflect the vast terrain that opens up once we begin to make use of the concept and vocabulary of epistemic rights. This book is intended as nothing more or less than gateway into that terrain.

1 What are epistemic rights?

The deliberate spread of false and misleading information about the opioid-based painkiller, OxyContin, by the pharmaceutical giant Purdue Pharma, has resulted in serious and indeed fatal harm. Many people have died. Many more continue to suffer. The case is notable both for the scale of the harm and for the complexity of the orchestrated misinformation campaign at its source. It is, however, far from anomalous. False and misleading advertising was, for example, fundamental to the devastating success of the tobacco industry in the 1950s and 60s (Proctor, 2011). Political misinformation and propaganda have been central to the success of political regimes throughout history. The spread of fake news, both historically and today, shares many of the characteristic features of these kinds of widespread and often coordinated misinformation efforts. The Purdue Pharma case serves as a useful basis for a discussion of epistemic rights not because it stands out but because it is, in some sense, archetypal.

Cases such as this are key to understanding epistemic rights and considering their role in complex, real world settings. As noted, I will discuss a range of cases throughout the book. In this first chapter, however, I answer the title question more directly by providing a definition and analysis of the concept of epistemic rights. What are epistemic rights? This is the foundational question of Chapter 1. As well as providing an answer to this question, I argue that epistemic rights are, first and foremost, a form of rights. I demonstrate that this is not as trivial as it sounds by contrasting my account of epistemic rights with a different notion of rights available in contemporary epistemology. Establishing that epistemic rights are as substantive as any other form of rights is key to establishing their significance in legal and moral discourse concerning rights.

In order to provide a substantive definition of epistemic rights, it will be helpful to break the foundational question down into two further questions. Firstly, what are *rights*? And secondly, what is it that makes them *epistemic*? These are the two focal questions of Chapter 1. When these questions have been answered, we will have a definition of epistemic rights to employ throughout the remainder of the book. It will then be possible to examine in more detail how epistemic rights operate in a variety of complex real world settings, such as the Purdue Pharma case.

What are rights?

The concept of rights is familiar in contemporary society, particularly in Western democracies where rights have accrued distinctive political force in the twentieth and twenty-first centuries. Especially notable is the emergence of declarations and covenants in the mid-twentieth century, seeking to articulate and enshrine a set of universal human rights, such as the *International Bill of Human Rights* (1948) and the *European Convention for the Protection of Human Rights and Fundamental Freedoms* (1950). The *International Bill of Human Rights* includes, for example, the right to 'life, liberty and security of person' (Article 3), the right to 'recognition as persons before the law' (Article 6) and the right to education (Article 26). The protection and promotion of human rights such as these are fundamental to the activism and advocacy work of political organisations like Amnesty International. Debates concerning the nature and efficacy of human rights comprise a significant cross-disciplinary literature (Freeman 2017; Donnelly and Whelan 2020; Smith 2020).

Beyond human rights, talk of rights finds a home in many spheres of public and private life. There are legal rights, determined by the legal system under which we live, such as the right to vote and the right to park in a parking space to which one owns a permit. Legal rights are, for many, distinct from moral rights, such as the right not to be discriminated against according to race or gender.[8] Legal and moral rights are often spoken about as political or cultural rights and carved into sub-categories such as women's rights, black rights,

---

8 The distinction between legal and moral rights is denied by legal positivists such as the nineteenth century philosopher Jeremy Bentham (1987 [1796]). For legal positivists, the only rights taken to exist are those established by legal codes. Bentham famously referred to the idea of moral or 'natural' rights as 'simple nonsense' (1987 [1796] p.53). There is not space to engage with the legal positivist position here and I will assume throughout the book that there are such things as moral rights. Note that neither the existence nor the contemporary significance of epistemic rights is affected if one adopts legal positivism, although the scope of the concept and of epistemic rights violations would naturally be narrower.

minority rights, worker's rights, LGBTQ rights, disability rights and so on. For those living under constitutional law, there are also constitutional rights, such as those outlined in the *Constitution of the United States*, including, for example, the Second Amendment right to 'keep and bear arms' and the Thirteenth Amendment right to freedom from slavery. In response to this diversity, rights theorising spans multiple disciplines including philosophy, politics and legal theory. A question central to rights theory is the question of what, if anything, unifies this diverse array such that we can sensibly refer to all of these as rights? In other words, what are rights?

I define a right as a *complex entitlement that provides justification for the performance and prohibition of actions and omissions*. I provide an analysis of the three distinct elements of this definition in the following sections. Firstly, I analyse the structure of rights and in doing so fill out the notion of a 'complex entitlement', drawing on the widely accepted insights of the legal philosopher, Wesley Hohfeld (1919). Secondly, I analyse the function of rights by addressing the question 'what do rights do?' Here, I unpack the part of the definition which states that a right 'provides justification for the performance and prohibition of actions and omissions'. Thirdly, I analyse the justification of rights by addressing the question 'why does a right-holder have a right?' Here, I focus on the part of the definition which states that a right 'provides justification'. These analyses substantiate the definition of a right as a complex entitlement that provides justification for the performance and prohibition of actions and omissions.

The structure of rights

The task of defining rights begins for many with an analysis of rights proposed by the legal philosopher, Wesley Hohfeld (1919). Hohfeld's early twentieth century work offers one of the best known contributions to the literature on rights and focuses on the structure of rights. Hohfeld identified systematic ambiguities in the use of the term 'rights' in legal contexts and sought to disambiguate these to provide greater clarity for the application of rights language in the law. In his own somewhat derisive terms, Hohfeld comments:

> chameleon-hued words are a peril both to clear thought and to lucid expression … inadequacy and ambiguity of terms unfortunately reflect, all too often, corresponding paucity and confusion as regards actual legal conceptions.
>
> (Hohfeld, 1919, p.29)

Hohfeld identified four aspects or senses of the term right, which he labelled *privileges, claims, powers* and *immunities*. Of these, Hohfeld maintained that only claims were rights "in the strictest sense" (p.30) according to a common understanding of rights in the law. In particular, Hohfeld highlighted the significance of the relationship between claims and duties. He noted that for every claim there is a correlative duty. In other words, if I have a claim, then someone else has a duty towards me either to act or not to act in a certain way. As Paul Graham (1996) puts it, "To possess a claim is to stand in a position legitimately to demand something from another, and the other is under a duty to perform the demanded action" (p.260). Claims determine what duties people have with respect to others' rights.

In contrast, privileges, powers and immunities have no such relationship with duties. These represent different senses of the term right but are not, according to Hohfeld, rights 'in the strictest sense'. Privileges remove any restrictions there might be on me doing something but they do not oblige me to do it nor place a duty on anyone else to help or hinder me.[9] Powers allow me to waive a claim that I have, in effect removing the duties placed on others by my claim. Immunities prevent others from taking away or altering the claims that I have and the duties that attach to them.

Property rights provide a useful example to illustrate these different senses of the term right (Wenar 2015). Take my mobile phone. I have a privilege-right to use my phone which means that there is nothing stopping me from using it. I have no duty not to use my phone. I also have a claim-right against you using my phone which means, for example, that I have the right to hide it from you or to ask you to stop using it and you have a duty not to use it without my permission. In addition, I have a power-right to allow you to use my phone, in which case, I waive my claim-right against you using it. Finally, I have an immunity-right which prevents you from taking away or altering my claim-right against you using it. You can't simply tell me that it is now your phone and expect me not to complain. These are the property rights that I have as a result of owning a phone. Each of these reflects a sense of the term right. Again, only claims, as the correlatives of duties, are rights

---

9 Some rights theorists use the term "liberty" in place of "privilege" when referring to this aspect of the Hohfeldian schema. I use the term privilege so that readers can more easily identify this notion in the original Hohfeldian text. Judith Jarvis Thomson (1990) provides an argument in favour of the term privilege in *The Realm of Rights* (pp.53–54).

'in the strictest sense' according to Hohfeld. I refer to the combination of these four senses of the term right as a *complex entitlement.*

I follow Hohfeld (1919) in regarding claims as the substantive notion that we are primarily concerned with when talking about rights. As such, most of the discussion in the book is about epistemic claim-rights. This focus on claim-rights brings the significance of duties to the fore. As Hohfeld emphasised, all claim-rights correlate to some duty owed to the right-holder. Such duties are called directed duties because they are directed towards a right-holder. As May (2015) notes, "Directed duties and claim-rights are, in effect, the same relation viewed from different perspectives" (p.524). This does not, however, mean that all directed duties entail claim-rights. I might have a duty to help you carry heavy shopping bags up the stairs, but it doesn't follow that you have a claim-right that I do so.

On the other hand, claim-rights do entail directed duties. As Cruft (2013) puts it, "directed duties are at the heart of rights" (p.201). For this reason, the examination of epistemic claim-rights requires the examination of epistemic directed duties and I will discuss both claim-rights and directed duties throughout the book. Note that, for simplicity, I refer to directed duties as duties. That is not to say that all duties are directed duties (see Sreenivasan 2010 for an account of non-directed duties). But directed duties, as the correlatives of Hohfeldian claim-rights, are my primary concern and, again for simplicity, I refer to these as duties throughout.

Given the focus that is placed on claim-rights, some additional terminology associated with claims is also worth noting. When speaking of claim-rights, rights theorists often speak of positive and negative rights. Positive rights are rights that pertain to what is done: rights to the *actions* of a duty-bearer. In other words, they require that a duty-bearer does something. Negative rights are rights that pertain to what is not done: rights to the *inaction* of a duty-bearer. In other words, they require that a duty-bearer does not do something. You might have a positive right that I make you a cup of tea, because I promised you that I would. You also have a negative right that I don't pour the tea over you when I bring it. Note that the inaction associated with negative rights is often referred to as an omission (especially in legal contexts) and I adopt this term throughout the book.

The distinction between positive and negative rights is important because rights are action-guiding. If I confuse a duty to do x with a duty not to do y, then I am misunderstanding what it is that the correlative right requires me to do (or not do). The right to free speech, for example, is not a positive right to be heard. It is a negative right not to be prevented from expressing one's views (Fried 1978, p.110). The man standing on a box and reading loudly from a religious text outside my office window does not have a positive right that I open my window and listen to what he has to say. He does have a negative right that I let him say it without interfering. Negative rights are sometimes referred to as rights to non-interference. Positive rights are rights to assistance.

To recap, a right is a complex entitlement, meaning that it is structured by the four senses of the term right that Hohfeld identified: privileges, claims, powers and immunities. This analysis of the structure of rights gives us an important piece of the puzzle but it is not the whole picture. It does not, for example, tell us what rights do. To explicate this, I now turn to the function of rights.

The function of rights

General consensus among rights theorists tells us that rights affect what we can and cannot permissibly do according to either morality or the law (or both). As such, rights correspond to *actions and omissions*. This point is worth emphasising in order to contrast it with the idea that rights correspond to, say, objects. I do not have a right to my mobile phone itself, rather, I have a right to actions regarding my phone, such as making a call or sending an email. My rights also correspond to the actions and omissions of other people regarding my phone. You are not permitted to make a call or send an email on it without my permission.

Lea Raible (2020) makes this point succinctly: "Conceptually speaking, rights mandate actions ... They need to provide reasons for others to act in a certain way" (p.50). This feature of rights has implications for the way that we talk about them. It is not uncommon to hear talk of rights to objects, goods, or services, for example, the right to food, education or healthcare. But, as Raible notes, "a right to a good is an imprecise expression of a right ... we need to translate 'food' into specific actions that form the content of the duty" (p.48). A person does not have the right to food itself, rather (if such a right exists) it is (at least) a negative right to non-interference with her obtaining and eating food and, arguably, a positive right to the provision of food by, for example, the State.

Rights to goods and services such as food and healthcare are more contentious than they might at first appear. This is precisely because we must translate the goods and services themselves into actions and omissions to be performed by particular duty-bearers. Like rights, duties pertain to actions and omissions. I return to this in Chapter 2. For easier reading, I will continue to speak of rights to goods, specifically epistemic goods and will remind the reader intermittently that this is essentially shorthand for rights to actions and omissions regarding those goods. The important point is that rights correspond to actions and omissions rather than objects, goods, or services. Thus, we have a basic answer to the question what do rights do? Rights mandate actions and omissions.

I call this a basic answer because it provides an essential insight regarding the function of rights but one that prompts a further iteration of the question. Rights mandate actions and omissions but what for? What function do such mandates have? Jarvis Thomson (1990) points us toward an answer in her observation that rights place constraints on behaviour (p.77). Rights affect what we can and cannot permissibly do according to either morality or the law (or both). In doing so, they *protect right-holders,* through their enforcement, from harm. Rights mandate actions and omissions and such mandates protect right-holders.[10]

The idea of rights providing protection can be seen in Mill's early and influential application of the concept of rights in *Utilitarianism* (1861):

> When we call anything a person's right, we mean that he has a valid claim on society to protect him in the possession of it, either by the force of law, or by that of education and opinion.
>
> (Mill, 1861, p. 36)

This articulation of rights helpfully captures two key components of the analysis of rights so far. Following Hohfeld (1919), I have asserted that rights 'in the strictest sense' are *claims* (and that they thereby establish duties). Now, by looking at the function of rights, I assert that rights mandate actions and omissions and in doing so *protect* right-holders. To paraphrase Mill, a right is a claim to protection.

This is not, however, the end of the story when it comes to the function of rights. One can place the idea that rights protect right-holders under further scrutiny. In particular, by asking the question '*in what sense* do rights protect right-holders?' Put another way, what is it about right-holders that is protected by rights? This issue deserves some attention in part because it attracted significant debate in the rights literature during the latter half of the twentieth century.

---

10 Note that a person is protected from harm when a potential harm to them is prevented from occurring through *either* the actions or omissions of others. Such protection may involve the *promotion* of their needs as well as the *prevention* of any active harms to them. In other words, they are protected when either their positive or negative rights are served.

Two prominent responses can be identified, both of which identify a core unifying function of rights.

The first response is commonly known as the Interest Theory of rights. The Interest Theory says that rights protect right-holders' interests. In other words, a person has a right when others have duties protecting that person's interests, often interpreted as their well-being. Mill (1861) was famously an Interest Theorist. He viewed moral rights as serving our natural interest in self-preservation and in doing so securing the basis of our existence. More recently, Raz (1984) has offered a prominent defence of the Interest Theory, expressed as follows:

> 'x has a right' if and only if x can have rights, and other things being equal, an aspect of x's well-being (his interest) is a sufficient reason for holding some other person(s) to be under a duty.
>
> (Raz, 1984, p.195)

According to Interest Theorists, such as Raz, duties are generated by rights in order to protect right-holders' interests, such as their well-being. In short, the function of rights is to protect the right-holder's interests.

The second response is commonly known as the Will Theory of rights. The Will Theory says that rights protect the right-holder's will. In other words, a person has a right when others have duties protecting that person's control over their free, autonomous choices. Kant (2013 [1797]) can be viewed as an inspiration for Will Theory in virtue of his contention that:

> There is only one innate right ... Freedom (independence from being constrained by another's choice), insofar as it can coexist with the freedom of every other in accordance with a universal law.
>
> (Kant, 2013 [1797], p.34)

Hart (1982) advanced the Will Theory of rights in the twentieth century. On his account, the central idea "is that of one individual being given by the law exclusive control, more or less extensive, over another person's duty" (p.183). A person who has a right can thus be considered a "small-scale sovereign" (p.183) regarding the actions and omissions that make up the correlative duty of the right. According to Will Theorists, such as Hart, duties are generated by rights in order to protect right-holders' control over their free, autonomous choices. In short, the function of rights is to protect the right-holder's will.

Do rights, including epistemic rights, serve to protect right-holders' interests or their will? The debate between Interest Theory and Will

Theory has occupied significant space in the rights literature and I am in no position to resolve it here. It is, moreover, unnecessary to pick a side. My goal is not to say anything radical or new about the function (or indeed the nature) of rights. Instead, I aim to draw attention to a previously under-examined class of rights. Both the Interest Theory and the Will Theory, along with various alternatives that have been proposed in recent years, are commensurate with that aim (for alternatives see Cruft 2004; Sreenivasan 2005; Wenar 2005). Indeed, I take it to be an advantage that I can remain essentially neutral with respect to different theories of rights. If epistemic rights exist, then any theory of rights should be able to accommodate them. Moreover, the ability to understand and apply the concept of epistemic rights should not be affected by which theory of rights one adopts. Having noted its place in the analysis of rights, I will, therefore, bracket the Interest versus Will theory debate. There persists a basic answer to the question of the function of rights: *rights mandate actions and omissions.*

To recap once more, a right is a complex entitlement that provides justification for the performance and prohibition of actions and omissions. A complex entitlement is a Hohfeldian combination of privileges, claims, powers and immunities. Along with Hohfeld, the aspect of this complex entitlement with which I am principally concerned is claims. The basic function of rights is to mandate actions and omissions. More precisely, they mandate the performance and prohibition of actions and omissions. In doing so, rights protect right-holders. This leaves a final component of the definition of rights to be analysed concerning the grounds or *justification of rights*. Rights mandate actions and omissions; they place constraints on behaviour. But what is it that grounds or justifies these constraints? Here, I turn to the part of the definition of rights that states that a right 'provides justification'.

The justification of rights

According to the definition, rights don't merely mandate the performance and prohibition of actions and omissions; they *provide justification* for the performance and prohibition of actions and omissions. Where does this justification come from? This is the question that one is concerned with when examining the justification of rights. An analogy will help to elucidate the question.

Road-signs mandate actions; they direct what we can and cannot permissibly do. In doing so, they protect us and others from harm. As with rights, however, they don't simply mandate actions, they also provide justification for doing so. That justification comes from something other than the road-sign itself. It is grounded in something more fundamental. If a person wants to know why they are being stopped from going the wrong way down a one-way street, one can simply point to the road-sign indicating that it is a one-way street and tell them what it means. But they may have further questions. Why does the existence of the road-sign dictate which way they are permitted to drive down the road? On what basis does a road-sign get to tell anyone what to do? Pointing back to the road-sign and reiterating what it means is unlikely to satisfy the person at this point. They are after something more fundamental. They want to know what the road-sign's apparent authority to determine their actions is based on.

When one is examining the justification of rights, one is in a similar position. One is looking for the more fundamental thing that imbues a person's right with sufficient authority to determine what other people can and cannot permissibly do. What is the 'rights' authority', so to speak, to mandate actions and omissions based on?

It is helpful to understand this aspect of the analysis of rights as addressing the question, why does a right-holder have a right? This is the 'why' of justification, rather than the 'why' of explanation. In other words, it asks what justifies any right-holder in their possession of a right and so in their authority to mandate the actions and omissions of others. Note that I am, for now, asking this question in a general sense: what justifies *any* right-holder in their possession of *any* right, rather than what justifies a particular right-holder in the possession of a particular right. This second question is the primary subject of Chapter 2.

Kamm (2007) offers an important insight with respect to the general question. She contends that rights "express the worth of the person rather than the worth of what is in the interests of that person" (p.271). Here, Kamm is explicitly contesting the Interest Theory but the central point she is making can be understood independently. Rights 'express the worth of the person'. It is the worth or value of right-holders that justifies their possession of rights. Put another way, having rights is part of what it means to have value for right-holders. As such, I maintain that rights are justified by the final value of right-holders. I say 'final value' here to indicate the sense in which the value that is expressed by rights is not itself derivative from some other valuable thing. Right-holders have final value: they are valuable in and of themselves.

Jarvis Thomson (1990) captures something of this when she writes "to have a right is to have a kind of moral status" (p.38). Similarly, Lomasky (1987) speaks of rights as "entitlement to moral space" (p.54). These assertions elucidate a view of rights that is sometimes called a 'status view'.[11] Status views ground the justification of rights in the status of right-holders. In other words, it is my status as a being of final value, that justifies my possession of rights. Nagel (1986, 1995), a prominent advocate of the status view, articulates it clearly:

> I believe it is most accurate to think of rights as aspects of status – part of what is involved in being a member of the moral community. The idea of rights expresses a particular conception of the kind of place that should be occupied by individuals in a moral system – how their lives, actions, and interests should be recognized by the system of justification and authorization that constitutes a morality.
>
> (Nagel, 1995, p.85)

It is the moral status of right-holders that justifies them in the possession of rights. In this sense, rights can be viewed as markers of moral status.

This status-based approach to the justification of rights is a non-instrumental approach. According to this non-instrumental approach, rights are justified in and of themselves. Contrast this with an instrumental approach to rights' justification, which sees the justification of rights as grounded in the further goods that they lead to. For example, one might think that rights are justified because they lead to an increase in overall happiness. If some other mechanism were found that led to an even greater increase in overall happiness, then, according to an instrumental approach, we could (and indeed should) dispense with the concept of rights in favour of this alternative. A non-instrumental approach denies this. Rights are justified by the final value of right-holders, even if respect for rights were to lead to, for example, a decrease in overall happiness. As Nagel (1995) puts it, "rights are a nonderivative and fundamental element of morality. They embody a form of recognition of each individual's value" (p.87).

Returning to the question, why does a right-holder have a right? I maintain that rights are justified by the final value of right-holders. In other words, a right-holder has a right because they are a being of final value. This is a status-based, non-instrumental justification of rights aligned with theorists such as Nagel (1995), Kamm (2007) and Cruft (2010).

This response to the justification of rights does not represent an end to our inquiry concerning rights justification, however. On the contrary,

---

11 Lomasky (1987) does not explicitly advance a status view but his expression of rights as entitlement to moral space is nonetheless pertinent.

as with most responses to this question, it raises further questions of its own. In particular, one must ask who qualifies as a being of final value and so as a right-holder: what kinds of beings or entities have rights? Once an answer has been found to this question, one must re-ask the original question in the particular. The answer so far tells us only what justifies right-holders in the possession of rights, in general. This does not explain the allocation of different rights to different right-holders at different times. In other words, once we know what kinds of beings or entities are right-holders, we must ask why any particular right-holder has any particular right. I take up both of these questions in Chapter 2. For now, I have provided a basic answer to the question of the justification of rights: rights are justified by the final value of right-holders.

This completes analyses of the three distinct components of the definition of rights, comprising the structure, function and justification of rights. Although this has required detailed analysis, it is worth noting that my approach is intended to be non-revisionary (Cruft 2004). In other words, I seek to provide an analysis of rights that makes sense of the concept that we typically find in ordinary language. In much the same way, I aim to provide an analysis of epistemic rights that makes sense of the concept in ordinary language. We do not currently use the phrase 'epistemic rights' in ordinary language but we do use derivative phrases, in particular 'the right to know'. I aim to provide an analysis of epistemic rights that ordinary language users of the phrase 'the right to know' (you and I, when we are not actively engaging in epistemology) would not find puzzling or alien. Indeed, one which ordinary language users would find familiar.

In order to make progress towards this goal, it has been necessary to traverse some complex terrain regarding the structure, function and justification of rights. In doing so, I have sought to substantiate the definition provided at the outset: a right is complex entitlement that provides justification for the performance and prohibition of actions and omissions. Principally, this definition tells us what rights are but the discussion so far also gives some clue as to why rights matter – why it is worth spending time thinking about rights and what significance rights have for right-holders.

Rights are significant for right-holders because they offer moral and legal protection against harmful actions and omissions and recourse to protest, complain or demand reparation. The recognition and enforcement of rights through political and legal codes and covenants demonstrates the significance of rights in contemporary society. We all have an interest, therefore, in determining what rights we have. The purpose of this book is to argue that some of our rights are epistemic rights. Moreover,

I seek to demonstrate the significance of epistemic rights for epistemic right-holders and for the wider communities in which they live. I have so far provided a definition of rights and an answer to the first of the two focal questions in this chapter: what are rights? I now turn to the second.

What makes a right an epistemic right?

The term 'epistemic right' is not one that appears often in discussions of rights or, indeed, in epistemology. Before locating the term in the landscape of contemporary epistemology, however, one must elucidate the word 'epistemic'. It bears remarking that seasoned epistemologists don't always agree on the meaning or use of this word. Nonetheless, I hope to provide a relatively uncontentious way of understanding it for present purposes. It is certainly worth pausing to consider the word, which represents a large sub-discipline of philosophy, both now and throughout philosophical history, and yet rarely makes an appearance outside academic settings. If epistemic rights are an important and often overlooked part of our lives, as I argue they are, then knowing what we are referring to when we talk about the epistemic is as important as knowing what we are referring to when we talk about rights. Indeed, understanding the word epistemic will go a long way towards answering the second focal question.

The word epistemic is derived from the ancient Greek word *epistēmē*, often translated as knowledge, sometimes as understanding. *Epistēmē* is derived from the ancient Greek verb *epistanai*, most commonly translated as 'to know or understand'. As such, the word epistemic is typically used by contemporary philosophers to refer to an array of states or goods related to the concept of knowledge. These include knowledge, truth, belief, justification, understanding, wisdom and information, as well as what one might think of as 'negative' states or goods such as misinformation and ignorance. A good way to understand the word epistemic, therefore, is to read it as a catch-all term relating to this collection of states or goods, as well as activities and experiences related to these, such as questioning, discovering and so on. This is how the word is typically used by contemporary philosophers.

I say typically because, within contemporary epistemology, the distinction between these different states or goods is often significant. In particular, the distinction between knowledge and belief is pertinent to many central debates in epistemology. As such, the word doxastic, derived from the ancient Greek word *doxa*, is sometimes used by epistemologists to refer specifically to belief as distinct from knowledge.

When doxastic is contrasted with epistemic, the word epistemic is usually being used to refer to knowledge, in particular, rather than to a range of goods. However, when the distinction between knowledge and belief is not immediately salient, epistemologists use the word epistemic in the way that I am suggesting, as a catch-all term for a range of states or goods, including belief. Given that the distinction between knowledge and belief is not immediately salient for present purposes, this is also the way that I use the word epistemic throughout the book.

Accordingly, to be an epistemic agent is to be someone (or perhaps something) who knows, believes, understands, can be justified, wise, informed, misinformed or ignorant. The epistemic domain is the domain of life concerned with these states or goods, as opposed to, for example, the aesthetic domain which is concerned with aesthetic states or goods such as beauty. Epistemology itself is the study of epistemic states or goods.

Throughout the book, I refer to knowledge, truth, belief, justification, understanding, wisdom, information, misinformation and ignorance as epistemic goods rather than states. It is worth noting that nothing much is meant to hang on this choice of term. That is not to say that the choice makes no difference. In fact, I think it does make a difference at a certain level of analysis. But that difference is not relevant for the present discussion and so I note here that the choice is primarily motivated by a desire for easy reading rather than anything else.

Nonetheless, the word good may seem like an odd choice to describe something like misinformation or ignorance, alongside goods such as knowledge and truth. In this context, however, good should be read as a synonym for product, rather than as the opposite to bad. The goods (products) that come off an assembly line in a factory might themselves be faulty or bad goods, so to speak. Likewise, in terms of epistemic goods, misinformation and ignorance might be just such faulty or bad goods (although perhaps not always). The analogy to assembly line products is helpful for interpreting the sense in which misinformation and ignorance can be classed as goods, even though they are often in some sense bad.

So, to reiterate, a good way to understand the word epistemic is to read it as a catch-all term relating to goods such as knowledge, truth, belief, justification, understanding, wisdom, information, misinformation and ignorance. Now that the term epistemic has been loosely defined, I can return to the focal question: what makes a right an epistemic right? As I said, understanding the word epistemic goes a long way towards answering this question.

I define an epistemic right as *a complex entitlement that provides justification for the performance and prohibition of actions and omissions concerning epistemic goods*. In answer to the focal question, then, a right is an epistemic right insofar as it concerns epistemic goods. Epistemic goods include knowledge, truth, belief, justification, understanding, wisdom, information, misinformation and ignorance. Thus, there is a straightforward answer to the focal question: what makes a right an epistemic right is the fact that it concerns epistemic goods such as these. The same can be said of other classes of rights. What makes a right a property right is the fact that it concerns property. Property rights are rights concerning property. Epistemic rights are rights concerning epistemic goods.[12]

With this in mind, it will help to offer further substance to the definition of epistemic rights. As before, I provide analyses of the three distinct elements of the definition comprising the structure, function and justification of epistemic rights. Given that epistemic rights are rights, much of the relevant work has already been done through the analysis of rights. Further detail will nonetheless help to substantiate the definition of epistemic rights.

The structure of epistemic rights

A right is a complex entitlement, meaning that it is structured by the four senses of the term right identified by Hohfeld (1919): privileges, claims, powers and immunities. How does this Hohfeldian structure translate to epistemic rights? In order to explicate these four senses of the term right, I gave an example in terms of the property rights that I have regarding my mobile phone. It will be helpful to see what such an example looks like in the case of epistemic rights.

Imagine that I am being tested for diabetes by my doctor. Once I have been tested, I have a privilege-right to know my blood-sugar levels which means that I have no duty not to know them. I also have a claim-right to know my blood-sugar levels meaning, for example, that I have a right to prevent my doctor from misinforming me about them and that my doctor has a duty to provide me with accurate results. In addition, I have a power-right to waive my claim-right and thereby not to know my blood-sugar levels. Finally, I have an immunity-right, which protects me from my doctor taking away or altering my claim-right to know my blood-sugar levels.

---

12 Notably, epistemic rights can also be property rights, as is the case with rights protecting intellectual property.

These four senses comprise the complex entitlement that I have regarding my blood-sugar levels after being tested for diabetes; they constitute my epistemic right regarding this information. As with rights in general, the aspect of the Hohfeldian complex entitlement that I am principally concerned with is epistemic claim-rights. Following Hohfeld's lead, epistemic claim-rights are understood as epistemic rights 'in the strictest sense'.

I examine epistemic claim-rights and the correlative epistemic duties in more detail in the coming chapters. Even this imagined case of the diabetes test raises many complex questions when transposed into real life. For now, however, it offers an insight into the structure of epistemic rights, illustrating how the Hohfeldian schema of privileges, claims, powers and immunities operates in the case of epistemic goods and so in the case of epistemic rights. Epistemic rights, like all other rights, comprise a complex entitlement of privileges, claims, powers and immunities.

The function of epistemic rights

My right to know my blood sugar levels after being tested for diabetes is an epistemic right, because it concerns information about my blood sugar levels – an epistemic good. This straightforward answer is complicated a little by considering the function of epistemic rights: what do epistemic rights do? In particular, recall that rights pertain to actions and omissions, as opposed to goods. Just as the right to food must be translated into the actions and omissions of particular duty-bearers regarding food, the right to information must be translated into the actions and omissions of particular duty-bearers regarding information. In the case of the diabetes test, my right to know my blood sugar levels, taken as a claim-right, translates to a duty on the part of my doctor to provide me with the accurate test results.

As before, then, this provides a basic answer to the question, what do epistemic rights do? Epistemic rights mandate actions and omissions concerning epistemic goods. Again, this is a basic answer because it prompts a further iteration of the question: what is the function of such mandates? One can again turn to the previous discussion; rights affect what we can and cannot permissibly do according to either morality or the law (or both). In doing so, they protect right-holders, through their enforcement, from harm. Epistemic rights mandate actions and omissions concerning epistemic goods and such mandates protect epistemic right-holders.

A further question still, concerns the particular sense in which epistemic rights protect epistemic right-holders. What is it about epistemic right-holders that is protected by epistemic rights? Here again, the Interest versus Will theory debate arises and, as before, I remain neutral with respect to that debate. One might think that epistemic rights protect the right-holder's epistemic interests or alternatively, that epistemic rights protect the right-holder's free, autonomous choices concerning epistemic goods. There is plenty of work to be done in spelling out the details of both. However, in either case, if epistemic rights exist and are like other classes of rights, then one's preferred theory of rights should be able to accommodate them and the ability to understand and apply the concept should not be affected by which theory one adopts.

Thus, the basic function of epistemic rights is to mandate actions and omissions concerning epistemic goods. More precisely, they mandate the performance and prohibition of actions and omissions concerning epistemic goods. In doing so, epistemic rights protect epistemic right-holders. This is the basic answer to the question, what do epistemic rights do? It leaves the third and final component of the definition of epistemic rights to be analysed, concerning the justification of epistemic rights.

The justification of epistemic rights

Epistemic rights don't merely mandate the performance and prohibition of actions and omissions concerning epistemic goods, they *provide justification* for doing so. The question of the justification of epistemic rights is, in the first instance, the question of where this justification comes from. As before, this is the question of why an epistemic right-holder has an epistemic right. That is the 'why' of justification, rather than the 'why' of explanation, and it is asked in general terms, rather than of any particular right-holder or any particular right.

According to the status view inspired by Kamm (2007), rights 'express the worth of the person'. In particular, it is the final value of right-holders that justifies their possession of rights. Rights are, therefore, justified by the final value of right-holders. As a class of rights, epistemic rights are justified in just the same way, by the final value of right-holders. However, given that epistemic rights are a particular class of rights, as opposed to rights in general, this explanation requires an additional layer of specificity. Thus, I maintain that epistemic rights are justified by the final value of right-holders *in the epistemic domain.*

What precisely does this mean? I will look in more detail at who or what counts as an epistemic right-holder in Chapter 2. The key point for now is that epistemic rights are justified by the final value of right-holders in a specific domain in much the same way as other classes of rights pertain to other specified domains. Property rights, for example, are justified by the final value of right-holders in the domain of property. In other words, these rights express the final value of the right-holder in relation to a particular domain. Epistemic rights express the final value of the right-holder in the epistemic domain. Again, I return to this in Chapter 2.

This basic explanation of the justification of epistemic rights, however, also clarifies a further important question concerning their nature. Are epistemic rights to be understood as a novel class of rights, distinct from legal and moral rights? The answer to this question is no. Epistemic rights, as I construe them, are also legal and/or moral rights. They form a distinct and unified class of rights because they are rights concerning epistemic goods. Just as property rights are a distinct and unified class of rights because they are rights concerning property. This doesn't mean that property rights are not also legal and/or moral rights. Nor does it mean that epistemic rights are not also legal and/or moral rights. They are; in fact, they must be. As Nagel (1995), succinctly puts it: "That people have rights of certain kinds which ought to be respected, is a moral claim that can be established only by moral argument" (p.85).

One can see this from the way in which epistemic rights are justified. I have said that epistemic rights are justified by the final value of right-holders in the epistemic domain. This explanation is based on the status view of rights from earlier, which says that it is the moral status of right-holders that justifies them in the possession of rights. In this sense, rights can be viewed as markers of moral status. The final value of right-holders, in whatever domain, is moral. This is as true for epistemic rights as for other rights. Epistemic rights are markers of *moral* status.

It does not follow from this that the epistemic domain collapses into the moral domain. There is, I believe, an epistemic domain distinct from the moral domain and we can talk about good epistemic conduct within this domain according to norms that are internal to it and so not reducible to moral norms. One might indeed think that moral and epistemic norms play distinct but interrelated roles in the case of epistemic rights. Moral norms are what justifies my right to information about my blood sugar levels, but epistemic norms dictate that my right is to true (rather than false) information.

Significantly, however, I think, along with Nagel (1995), that the notion of a *right* is a moral notion. Rights provide justification for the performance and prohibition of actions and omissions in order to protect right-holders from harm. This function is a moral function, even when the harm is epistemic. The point is that, if a person is to be protected from epistemic (or any) harm by a right, then it is because of their *moral* status. That is why epistemic rights are markers of moral status. Once you attach the epistemic to the notion of rights, you enter the moral domain. Thus, epistemic rights are not to be viewed as a novel class of rights in addition to legal and moral rights. They are, nonetheless, a distinct, unified and important class of rights.

I have offered a status-based, non-instrumental justification of epistemic rights. As before, this leaves much to be said about what kinds of beings or entities have epistemic rights and about how to allocate particular epistemic rights to particular right-holders. These issues are explored in Chapter 2. For now, I have provided a basic answer to the question of the justification of epistemic rights: epistemic rights are justified by the final value of right-holders in the epistemic domain.

Building on the previous discussion, this completes analyses of the structure, function and justification of epistemic rights. Through these analyses, I have added further substance to the definition of an epistemic right understood as a complex entitlement that provides justification for the performance and prohibition of actions and omissions concerning epistemic goods. I have also highlighted gaps in the explication so far, which will be filled in the remaining chapters.

In addition, the discussion has indicated something of the significance of epistemic rights. Epistemic rights are significant for right-holders because they offer moral and legal protection against harmful actions and omissions concerning epistemic goods and recourse to protest, complain or demand reparation. If my doctor misinforms me about my blood sugar levels, then I can complain about it and demand reparation as well as the accurate test results. Much as I can complain and demand payment from you if you run up a large bill using my phone without my permission. This is an important point to emphasise. Epistemic rights are significant to right-holders because they are rights in both the fullest and the strictest sense: they comprise all aspects of the Hohfeldian (1919) schema, including claims.

Having answered the two focal questions of this chapter, we now have a definition of epistemic rights to work with for the remainder of the book. I have answered the foundational question of Chapter 1: what are epistemic rights? Epistemic rights are complex entitlements that provide justification for the performance and prohibition of actions and omissions concerning epistemic goods. The analytical task is essentially complete.

This last point about the significance of epistemic rights to right-holders, however, brings into focus an important dimension of the analytical task still to be addressed in full. I said at the start that epistemic rights are a form of rights and noted that this is not as trivial as it sounds. Recognition of epistemic rights as rights, in both the fullest and the strictest sense according to the Hohfeldian schema is key to appreciating the non-trivial nature of the claim that epistemic rights are rights. I will end the chapter by examining this claim in more detail. In essence, this involves asking whether epistemic rights are really *rights*. As well as filling out the non-trivial definition of epistemic rights, this will help to lay the groundwork for an investigation of epistemic rights violations and the harms that they cause in Chapters 3 and 4.

Are epistemic rights really rights?

A right is a complex entitlement that provides justification for the performance and prohibition of actions and omissions. A complex entitlement comprises the full Hohfeldian schema of privileges, claims, powers and immunities. Epistemic rights can likewise be understood according to this schema. As such, epistemic rights are akin to rights in other domains, such as property: epistemic rights are as substantive as any other rights.

This is how I propose to understand the notion of epistemic rights. This way of understanding epistemic rights, however, differs from one found implicitly in a related but orthogonal philosophical literature concerning the 'right to believe' (James 1896; Conee 1987; Feldman 1988; Alston 1989; Audi 1991; Adler 2002; Ginsborg 2007). The term 'epistemic rights' is not typically employed in this literature nor is the right to believe placed within a broader framework of rights. Nonetheless, this body of work comprises a relatively significant literature in epistemology in which the notion of a right is in operation and, as such, it is worth locating the current discussion of epistemic rights in relation to that literature.

Debates in the right to believe literature revolve around the question of what it means for a belief to be justified. What justifies my belief that the sky is blue, for example? Put in the terms of the debate, what gives me the 'right to believe' that the sky is blue? In this literature, the question of whether or not I have the right to believe is, therefore, the question of whether or not I am justified in believing. Do I, for example, have good reasons or evidence for believing that the sky is blue? If so, then one might say that I have the right to believe it. As such, having a right to believe is akin to having justification for believing.

In contrast, the question of whether I am justified in believing that the sky is blue is, for my purposes, irrelevant to the question of whether I have the right to believe that the sky is blue. It is not my justification – my reasons or evidence, say – for believing that the sky is blue that determines whether or not I have the right to believe it. If I have the right, I have it regardless of my justification and, indeed, even if I have no justification for believing that the sky is blue or have justification for believing that it is not blue. Having a right to believe, in this sense, is not akin to having justification for believing, it is akin to having a right to use one's mobile phone. It should be clear that these are two quite different conceptions.

To draw out the contrast, it is helpful to look at James' (1869) canonical essay, *The Will to Believe*, in which he discusses justification for religious belief. This essay constitutes an early and seminal contribution to the literature concerning the right to believe. James describes *The Will to Believe* as no less than "an essay in justification of faith, *a defence of our right* to adopt a believing attitude in religious matters" (p.1, emphasis added). In the essay, James argues that belief in a god is justified and he views this as a defence of the right to believe in a god. A person's right to believe is, therefore, closely bound to their justification for believing. This tight connection has persisted in contemporary debates concerning the right to believe.

A closer look at the James quotation is illuminating, however. James (1896) argues for a justification of faith, not in order to *establish* the right to believe in a god but in order to *defend it*. As such, the justification of faith that he offers does not *give* someone the right to believe in a god. Rather, James suggests that this right to believe is under attack. The task of providing justification for this belief is a way of defending that right. Specifically, James is defending the right to believe in a god against the charge that such a belief is irrational or unjustified. It is for this reason that the question of whether or not a person is justified in believing is relevant.

The question of whether or not a person is justified in believing, however, is not always clearly distinguished from the question of whether or not a person has the right to believe. Arguably the language of rights is altogether misleading in the contemporary literature for precisely this reason. At any rate, it is helpful to see that the right to believe, as I construe it, has little to do with justification for belief. Rather, I understand the right to believe in terms of a Hohfeldian complex entitlement. Again, this treatment of the notion of rights differs significantly from that found in the right to believe literature. This difference is brought out explicitly in the work of Leif Wenar (2003). Wenar is one scholar who actually uses the term epistemic rights in the right to believe literature. He does so in order to contrast the right to believe with legal rights. Wenar argues that, unlike legal rights, the right to believe is only ever a privilege-right. As such, having the right to believe that the sky is blue amounts to having no duty not to believe it. Notably, Wenar switches from talk of duties to talk of 'conclusive reasons' when discussing the right to believe. Thus, he says that the privilege-right to believe amounts to having no conclusive reason not to believe (2003, p.142).

Consequently, while Wenar does consider the right to believe in relation to other classes of rights, as I am doing, he marks it out as more restricted. This is an important difference. Wenar's notion of epistemic rights is more restricted than the one I am employing in three key respects. Firstly, Wenar explicitly and exclusively identifies epistemic rights with rights to believe. In contrast, I construe epistemic rights as extending beyond rights to believe, encompassing rights to know, understand, be informed and so on.

Secondly, Wenar restricts epistemic rights to privilege-rights. Notably, for example, in his *Stanford Encyclopedia of Philosophy* entry on 'Rights' (2015), Wenar comments, "It is interesting to consider, why [the] epistemic ... [realm] contain[s] no claims, powers, or immunities" (Section 5.5). In contrast, I maintain that epistemic rights include the full Hohfeldian schema. My right to know my blood-sugar levels, after being tested for diabetes, is more than the mere absence of a duty on my part not to know them: a privilege right. Most importantly, it is a claim-right.

Thirdly, Wenar talks of conclusive reasons to believe or not to believe, as opposed to duties. Combined with the fact that he restricts epistemic rights to privilege-rights, this indicates that Wenar is not conceiving of rights in the epistemic domain as rights in either the fullest or the strictest sense according to the Hohfeldian schema. In other words, as rights proper. Duties are central to the Hohfeldian schema: claim-rights correlate with duties and privilege-rights are defined by the absence of duty. Switching from talk of duties to talk of conclusive reasons is, therefore, indicative of a conception of rights that does not map onto the Hohfeldian schema.

To reiterate, then, epistemic rights as I construe them are as substantive as any other form of rights. Epistemic rights as they are construed explicitly by Wenar (2003, 2015) and implicitly in the wider right to believe literature, are not rights in either the fullest or the strictest sense. It is, however, important to note that these are not two competing conceptions of epistemic rights in any meaningful sense. Wenar and others contributing to the right to believe literature are essentially having a different conversation to the one that I am pressing for in this book. As such, my goal is not to usurp or undermine the notion of rights that is in operation in that literature. I do, however, hope to forestall any potential conflation between two different uses of the notion of rights in the epistemic domain. Contrasting these different uses has, moreover, allowed me to emphasise the substantive nature of epistemic rights, as I construe them, and to demonstrate the sense in which epistemic rights are rights in both the fullest and the strictest sense. Epistemic rights really are rights. This concludes the analysis of epistemic rights.

Summary

In this chapter, I have been concerned with the analytical question: what are epistemic rights? I have offered a philosophical analysis drawing on the extant rights literature and have applied conclusions reached there regarding the structure, function and justification of rights to the epistemic domain. Thus, an epistemic right is a complex entitlement that provides justification for the performance and prohibition of actions and omissions concerning epistemic goods. I have positioned this analysis in relation to an orthogonal debate in epistemology concerning the right to believe and have argued that epistemic rights are as substantive as any other form of rights.

As noted, nothing I have said is intended to be revisionary. Rather the aim is to draw attention to an under-examined, distinct and unified class of rights. While some of the ground covered in this chapter has been necessarily technical, the concept of epistemic rights, once understood, should be both familiar and easy to deploy in ordinary language. In concise and general terms, epistemic rights are those rights that protect and govern the quality, distribution and accessibility of epistemic goods. The right to know, to be informed, to have the truth and so on. It is not hard to see these rights in operation in the Purdue Pharma case. It is, moreover, valuable to view that case, and others that will be discussed in due course, through the lens of epistemic rights. Thus, having completed the analytical task, we now turn attention to the more overtly political task of deciphering who, in particular, has epistemic rights.

2   Who has epistemic rights?

In 2013, CIA intelligence analyst Edward Snowden copied and leaked a large amount of highly classified information to journalists at *The Guardian* and *The Washington Post*, whilst working as a contractor at the US National Security Agency (NSA). The information revealed details of top secret surveillance programmes run by the NSA, involving the US, the UK, Canada and Australia, in cooperation with international telecommunications companies. *The Guardian* and *The Washington Post* ran a series of headline stories exposing the existence of these programmes, detailing the collection of extensive information on citizens' personal communications.[13, 14] The leaked information and the exposed surveillance programmes quickly became the subject of intense national and international debate.

Controversy and conspiracy abound in relation to the Snowden case. On the one hand, the handling of the leaked information has been widely praised in professional media circles. Journalists at *The Guardian* and *The Washington Post* were honoured with the George Polk Award for National Security Reporting in 2013, an award which they dedicated to Snowden.[15] The newspapers were also awarded a joint Pulitzer Prize for Public Service in 2014, for helping "to spark a debate about the relationship between the government and the public over issues of security and privacy".[16] Following this, *The Guardian's* chief editor, Alan Rusbridger, Tweeted that it sent a "powerful message" about Snowden's act of public service.[17]

13 https://www.theguardian.com/world/2013/jun/06/nsa-phone-records-verizon-court-order [Accessed 6 Feb 2020].
14 http://www.washingtonpost.com/wp-srv/special/national/nsa-timeline/ [Accessed 6 Feb 2020].
15 https://www.liu.edu/George-Polk-Awards/Articles/2013-Winners [Accessed 6 Feb 2020].
16 https://www.pulitzer.org/prize-winners-by-year/2014 [Accessed 6 Feb 2020].
17 https://twitter.com/arusbridger/status/455784353457778688 [Accessed 6 Feb 2020].

In contrast, the official position of the US government has been unflinchingly punitive. Eighteen days after the initial reports, the US revoked Snowden's passport. The following day Snowden flew from Hong Kong, where the initial leak took place, to Moscow where he has since been granted asylum. In June 2013, US federal prosecutors charged Snowden with theft of government property and two counts of violating the Espionage Act of 1917. Mirroring these opposing stances, public opinion on Snowden himself has been divided with views ranging from traitor and spy to patriot and hero.[18]

Controversy surrounding Snowden and the NSA leaks turns implicitly on the question of *who has the right to know what*. As such, this controversy captures the essence of the question in the title of this chapter. One can ask, for example, if governments have the right to read, listen to and track the private communications of law-abiding citizens or if law-abiding citizens have a right to privacy. If Snowden, or the journalists he approached, had a right (or a duty) to disclose the classified documents and if the public has a right to know about the mass surveillance activities of its government. These are just some of rights-related questions that have featured centrally, if at times implicitly, in the national and international debate, following the leak.

Cases such as this give rise to numerous iterations of the question, who has the right to know what? Despite the complexities of these cases, the question itself is deceptively simple. On its simplest reading, it has an equally simple answer: everyone. Everyone has epistemic rights. This simple answer, however, masks a more complex picture. Whistleblowing cases, like that of Snowden, help to illustrate the nuances and complexities of this picture.

In order to examine this complex picture, as with the previous chapter, it will help to break the title question down into two (again, deceptively simple) focal questions. First, who *can* have epistemic rights? Second, who *does* have epistemic rights? In combination, these questions ask why any particular epistemic right-holder has any particular epistemic right. As such, they concern the allocation of epistemic rights. In addition, the same questions must be asked with respect to the allocation of epistemic duties. When these questions have been answered, an enriched account of epistemic rights will have been provided, facilitating a deeper understanding of its applications in real-world scenarios, such as the Snowden case.

18 https://www.washingtonpost.com/news/worldviews/wp/2014/01/03/the-three-types-of-nsa-snooping-that-edward-snowden-revealed/?arc404=true [Accessed 6 Feb 2020].

Who can have epistemic rights?

I said that the title question of this chapter has a deceptively simple answer: everyone has epistemic rights. This simple answer is complicated by the first focal question: who *can* have epistemic rights? In essence, this question asks what is required in order to qualify as an epistemic right-holder. Do babies or people in a deep coma have epistemic rights? Do past and future humans have epistemic rights? Do animals or artificially intelligent machines have epistemic rights? In other words, who counts as 'everyone'?

Addressing this question builds on the basic account of the justification of epistemic rights in Chapter 1. There I argued that epistemic rights, in general, are justified by the final value of right-holders in the epistemic domain. I noted, however, that this doesn't tell us how to justify the allocation of particular epistemic rights to particular right-holders. This is the explicit target of Chapter 2. In order to arrive at an answer, one must first carve out the domain of epistemic right-holders itself. In other words, one must determine what it takes to be an epistemic right-holder. This is the target of the first focal question.

There is a simple answer available to this question too. It is clear, after all, that all epistemic right-holders are right-holders. Epistemic rights just are a form of rights. Moreover, epistemic rights express the final value of right-holders in the epistemic domain. So, epistemic right-holders are simply right-holders in the epistemic domain. Just as property right-holders are right-holders in the domain of property. You are a property right-holder if you are a right-holder and the right you hold concerns property. Likewise, you are an epistemic right-holder if you are a right-holder and the right you hold concerns epistemic goods. This simple answer, however, leads directly to a more difficult question: what does it take to be a right-holder? As such, the present task aligns with the task of determining who or what counts as a right-holder.

This task has, naturally, occupied a portion of the literature on rights (Feinberg, 1980; Partridge, 1981; Lomasky, 1987; Hartney, 1991; Regan, 1992; Wellman, 1995). One common notion posits the necessity of mental states and/or mental functioning for the ascription of rights. Feinberg (2013), for example, contrasts conscious beings with 'mere things', albeit things of great value, such as the Taj Mahal:

> mere things have no conative life; neither conscious wishes, desires, and hopes; nor urges and impulses; nor unconscious drives, aims,

goals; nor latent tendencies, directions of growth, and natural fulfillments.

(Feinberg, 2013, p.374)

As such, according to Feinberg and others, mere things cannot be right-holders. The same is true of epistemic rights: mere things cannot be epistemic right-holders. Rocks, sunsets and buildings do not qualify as epistemic right-holders: they do not have epistemic rights.[19] At the other end of the spectrum, you and I do qualify as epistemic right-holders. We are right-holders and some of our rights concern epistemic goods. Building on the idea that mental states and/or mental functioning are necessary for the ascription of rights, one tempting route for determining who can have epistemic rights is to look to epistemic states and/or 'epistemic functioning'. This route says that epistemic right-holders are those beings or entities with the capacity for epistemic states: beings that can know, believe, understand and so on. This is one way of explaining why you and I qualify as epistemic right-holders, while rocks and sunsets and buildings do not; the latter do not have the capacity for epistemic states. In Chapter 1, I referred to beings who can know, believe understand and so on as epistemic agents. Thus, one might conclude that in order to have epistemic rights, one must be an epistemic agent. I will argue that this tempting conclusion, however, is false.

Epistemic rights and epistemic capacity

An epistemic agent is someone (or perhaps something) who can know, believe, understand and so on. As such, epistemic agents have 'epistemic capacity': the capacity to be in an epistemic state. If being an epistemic agent is required in order to be an epistemic right-holder, then any beings or entities who are not epistemic agents, and so lack epistemic capacity, must also fail to qualify as epistemic right-holders. A new-born baby, for example, does not appear to have the capacity to know anything. Knowing and believing are arguably states that emerge in young children and not before. As such, if epistemic capacity is a requirement for epistemic rights, babies cannot qualify as epistemic right-holders. They lack epistemic capacity and so they cannot have epistemic rights.

---

19 The debate concerning the rights of 'mere things' is more controversial when it comes to consideration of, for example, AI machines. I return to this in due course.

For some, this conclusion may seem unobjectionable. Babies cannot come to know or understand so how can they have rights to knowledge and understanding? Imagine, for example, a baby rather than an adult being tested for diabetes. It would seem odd to say that the baby has a right to know her blood sugar levels after being tested for diabetes precisely because she cannot come to know them. Seeming odd, however, is not the same as being false. Despite it indeed seeming odd, I contend that it is true, just as in the adult case, that a baby has the right to know her blood sugar levels after being tested for diabetes.

The oddness of this can be explained, in part, by recalling the qualification made in Chapter 1 concerning the function of rights. Rights pertain to actions and omissions, rather than to goods and services (or anything else). Consequently, talk of rights to goods and services should be taken as short-hand for talk of rights to actions and omissions that, for example, secure those goods and services for right-holders. Likewise, talk of the right to know should be taken as short-hand for talk of the right to actions and omissions that, for example, produce or result in knowledge for right-holders. Saying that a baby has the right to know her blood sugar levels after being tested for diabetes is, therefore, short-hand for saying that the baby has a right to actions and omissions that result in knowledge of her blood sugar levels for her.

That said, the phrase 'actions and omissions that result in knowledge of her blood sugar levels for her', warrants further explanation. One can relatively easily make sense of the notion of actions and omissions that result in knowledge of blood sugar levels. These are the actions and omissions of the healthcare professionals involved in the blood sugar tests requiring them to, for example, perform the tests responsibly and communicate the results truthfully. But what does it mean for these actions and omissions to result in knowledge of a baby's blood sugar levels *for her*, given that the baby cannot herself come to know? Again, the relationship between the baby's epistemic capacity and her epistemic rights appears salient.

Indeed, it is salient. A person's epistemic capacity does interact with their epistemic rights. This interaction between rights and capacities further explains, why talk of a baby's right to know her blood sugar levels seems odd. Such talk amounts to granting the baby a right that she does not have the capacity to exercise. Again, however, seeming odd is not the same as being false. In fact, a baby's inability to know her blood sugar levels does not take away or limit her right to know them. She has the right regardless of her capacity. This is because, while capacities do interact with rights, a person's rights are not *determined* by their capacities.

This is true of rights in general. A wheelchair user retains the right to walk although he may not have the capacity to do so. We can see this by imagining a scenario (perhaps a near-future scenario) in which technology is developed that enables a particular wheelchair user to walk. He wouldn't suddenly acquire the right to walk under these circumstances simply in virtue of being able to do so. He already has that right. New technology might allow him to exercise the right in a way that he previously couldn't but having the capacity to walk doesn't itself determine whether or not he has the right to. The reverse is also true. Fifteen-year-olds in the UK and convicted felons serving prison sentences in most US states have the capacity to vote, but they do not have the right to. Rights are not determined by capacities.

Much like a wheelchair user's right to walk, the same can be said of a baby's right to know her blood sugar levels after being tested for diabetes. If, in an admittedly more fanciful scenario, some kind of cognitive technology was developed that enabled babies to come to know complex things, then the baby in our doctor's office might be able to exercise her right to know her blood sugar levels in a way that she previously couldn't. But the ability-bestowing technology itself does not determine whether or not the baby has the right to know her blood sugar levels. She already has that right.

The sense in which a person's capacity interacts with their rights is, therefore, not to grant them or take them away. Rather, this interaction establishes the need for proxies that can stand-in for right-holders as well as institutions that can enforce rights on behalf of right-holders who cannot enforce their own. In either case, the right itself is not transferred to the proxy or to the institution – they do not *become* the right-holder. In the case of the baby being tested for diabetes, her parents or carers will be required to act as epistemic proxies on her behalf. If they fail to do so, the relevant health and social care institutions will be required to enforce the baby's rights and hold her proxies to account. Crucially, though, it is the *baby's* rights that are exercised and enforced by her proxies and the relevant supporting institutions.

O'Neill (1988) captures the significance of this in the case of children:

> Children easily become victims. If they had rights, redress would be possible. Rather than being powerless in the face of neglect, abuse, molestation and mere ignorance they (like other oppressed groups) would have legitimate and (in principle) enforceable claims against others. Although they (unlike many other oppressed groups) cannot claim their rights for themselves, this is no reason for denying them rights. Rather it is reason for setting

up institutions that can monitor those who have children in their
charge and intervene to enforce rights.

(O'Neill, 1988, p.445)

Children and babies are right-holders because they are beings of final
value, not because they have any particular capacities. Their rights
express their value. As such, children and babies are right-holders
even though they are often incapable of exercising their rights, just
as in the diabetes case. In this case, the right concerns an epistemic
good and so it is an epistemic right. The fact that the good is epistemic
does not take away the right or diminish the significance of exercising
and enforcing it on behalf of the baby. That the baby lacks epistemic
capacity, in fact, only emphasises the necessity of proxies and care-
taking institutions that can enforce her epistemic rights on her behalf.
Children and babies have epistemic rights.[20]

The same can be said of other cases involving lack of capacity. One
might think it odd to ascribe epistemic rights to someone in a deep
coma given that they seemingly cannot come to know, believe, understand and so on. But, just as in the case of babies, this lack of capacity
does not take away or diminish the person's rights. Rather, it establishes the need for epistemic proxies and the relevant institutions capable of exercising and enforcing their rights on their behalf. In the case
of a person in a deep coma, this might involve, for example, informing
relatives of their condition and accurately recording their brain activ-
ity. Far from them not having a right to this information, it is, in fact,
essential that *their right* to this information is upheld.

This can be seen perhaps even more starkly in the case of those
suffering from cognitive ageing disorders, such as dementia. A characteristic feature of such disorders is to reduce a person's cognitive
capacities over time, including their ability to know and understand.
Notably, a person suffering from dementia does not lose the ability to
know and understand all at once (or entirely), as a person in a deep
coma may do. If epistemic rights were determined by epistemic capacities, then a person suffering from dementia would gradually lose their
epistemic rights over time in accordance with their ability to know,
understand and so on.

---

20 Some rights theorists, such as Hart (1955), hold that babies and infants are not
   right-holders because they do not have an autonomous, independent will. This
   aspect of the Will Theory has come under significant criticism in the literature and,
   as with the Will vs Interest theory debate, I will bracket it.

In both legal and moral terms, this would amount to taking away a person's epistemic rights on the basis of their cognitive health. But deterioration in health shouldn't (and doesn't) take away a person's rights, epistemic or otherwise. If anything, as noted, it highlights the necessity of the proxies and institutions that exist to ensure that *their rights* are exercised and enforced. This is as true for epistemic rights as for any other form of rights. A person's epistemic rights are not determined by their epistemic capacities. The tempting conclusion from earlier is false: epistemic right-holders do not have to be epistemic agents with epistemic capacity.

If not epistemic capacity, then what?

Denying the conclusion that epistemic right-holders must have epistemic capacity and so be epistemic agents leads back to the original focal question: who can have epistemic rights? In particular, if one does not limit the class of epistemic right-holders to the class of epistemic agents, then how does one define this class? Here, I refer again to the simple answer offered earlier: epistemic right-holders are right-holders in the epistemic domain. In other words, you qualify as an epistemic right-holder if you qualify as a right-holder and the right you hold concerns epistemic goods. To reiterate, then, the challenging question is the question of what qualifies one as a right-holder in the first place. This is a question shared by rights-theorists across the board.

In addition to the cases just discussed, several other hard cases confront those attempting to answer this question. I have said that rights express the final value of right-holders. It is this final value that provides a basic justification for rights, including epistemic rights. How do we determine who or what is a being of final value? To begin, it seems likely that all presently existing humans are beings of final value. Recall that final value is a kind of non-derivative, basic value: a thing that is finally valuable is valuable in and of itself. I take it to be incumbent upon anyone who wishes to deny that all presently existing humans are finally valuable, to make an argument for this. If one accepts that all presently existing humans are finally valuable, then, given that rights express right-holders' final value, this suggests that all presently existing humans qualify as right-holders. Beyond this, harder cases start to emerge.

Take, for example, past and future humans. Do we continue to have rights after we cease to exist, or have them before we come to exist? This question adds a wrinkle of complexity, which has been discussed in the rights literature (Lomasky, 1987; Feinberg, 2013; Partridge, 1981).

We often act as if both the dead and future generations do have rights: life insurance companies pay out after death, activists campaign for the rights of future generations to clean air, water and so on. One might argue that future generations also have rights to education and the results of current scientific research. If so, then they appear to have rights concerning epistemic goods: epistemic rights. It is, however, difficult to make sense of the notion of right-holders that do not presently exist. Who or what is the right-holder in these cases? Nonetheless, if we view past and future humans as finally valuable, then, according to the basic justification of rights, they qualify as right-holders.

What about non-humans? The debate over animal rights has been one of the liveliest and most contentious in the rights literature (Frey, 1977; Narveson, 1987; Regan, 1992; Singer, 1995; Cohen, 1997). Regan (1992) offers a thorough defence of animal rights on the basis that animals "bring the mystery of a unified psychological presence to the world. Like us, they possess a variety of sensory, cognitive, conative and volitional capacities" (p.xvi). Regan establishes a baseline for the ascription of rights, along the lines of mental functioning. Critics, however, contend that this baseline is too low; wherever we draw the line, it should exclude the possibility of rights for non-human animals (Frey, 1977; Narveson, 1987; Cohen, 1997). Alternatively, in his seminal contribution, Singer (1995) rejects outright the use of a rights framework for grounding the moral status of animals. Nonetheless, as with past and future humans, it seems plausible (perhaps more so), that we view animals as finally valuable. If so, this suggests that animals also qualify as right-holders.

Of course, animals are not the only non-humans to consider. Advances in artificial intelligence (AI) have brought ethical questions about the use of AI to the fore in recent years. As AI becomes increasingly sophisticated, questions about how we interact with and treat AI machines become increasingly salient. Should we be permitted to verbally abuse AI home assistants or act violently towards near-future AI robots in the street? If not, why not? Is there a point at which AI machines become right-holders? One might be tempted to think that such a point is a conceptual impossibility. However advanced, AI machines will always be machines and machines can only ever have instrumental as opposed to final value. There might still be good reasons not to verbally or physically abuse them but those reasons are not derived from the final value of the machines themselves. If they cannot have final value, then they cannot have rights. Much interesting philosophical discussion lies here, beyond the scope of the current project.

There is no space to address any of these complex questions in sufficient depth. It is, however, worth noting the serious moral and legal significance of the questions themselves. Human societies have consistently failed to grant rights to legitimate right-holders throughout history: children, women, black people, disabled people, LGBTQ and so on. Given this track record, it would be unwise to dismiss the possibility of, for example, AI rights without serious consideration. Mary Wollstonecraft's exasperated appeal in *A Vindication of the Rights of Woman* (2004 [1792]), over 200 years ago, appears remarkably apt in this regard: "if they be really capable of acting like rational creatures, let them not be treated like slaves" (p.35). Wollstonecraft was seeking to establish the moral status of women as equal to men. In much the same way, we would need to establish the moral status of AI as equal to humans (and all other right-holders), in order to grant AI rights. In other words, we would need to establish the final rather than merely instrumental value of AI.

The key point is that, in all these hard cases, the question of whether or not a being or entity can have epistemic rights is settled by answering the question of whether or not they can have rights. The task of determining who or what counts as an epistemic right-holder aligns with the task of determining who or what counts as a right-holder. As noted, this task has taken up a notable portion of the rights literature. The hard cases discussed in that debate are also hard cases here and there is not space to explore any one of them in depth. Happily, if you already have a position on who qualifies as a right-holder, you can apply this to the question of who can have epistemic rights. If not, then you must acknowledge, along with other rights-theorists, that challenges remain with respect to that question.

Either way, the discussion of this first focal question has not been futile. I have ruled out one tempting route for determining who can have epistemic rights, which tied epistemic rights to epistemic capacity. Moreover, I have again highlighted the alignment between epistemic rights and other rights: epistemic rights are as substantive as any other rights. As such, the task of determining who can have epistemic rights is relevant for both rights-theorists and epistemologists.

This alignment is important. The question of who can have epistemic rights should not be confined to the purely epistemic arena or reduced to questions about epistemic capacity and epistemic agency. Nor should it be the subject of purely epistemological debate, without input from political, legal and moral theory. Denying or limiting a person's rights is a serious business. Such business is rightly conducted in the legal and moral domains. Denying epistemic rights to babies, infants, people in deep comas, dementia sufferers and so on requires moral and/or legal justification. As O'Neill (1988) stresses in the case of children, groups such as these can easily become victims. This provides all the more reason to recognise and defend their rights, including their epistemic rights, and all the more reason for caution when it comes to denying epistemic rights to any group or, indeed, to individuals. All right-holders can have epistemic rights.

Who does have epistemic rights?

All right-holders can have epistemic rights. But not all right-holders have the same epistemic rights. I have a right to know my blood sugar levels after being tested for diabetes; you don't have a right to know them. The allocation of particular epistemic rights to particular right-holders is, like all rights, conditional on certain things such as who, when and where the right-holder is. So, who does have epistemic rights? This is the second focal question of the chapter. Of course, for any individual, the possible sets of circumstances that may be relevant for determining the allocation of epistemic rights will be vast. The task here is not to assess every set of circumstances in every possible case, but to determine a general heuristic or rule that can be applied to all cases: a rule for the allocation of epistemic rights. The second focal question is therefore answered by examining how we determine who has epistemic rights. A general heuristic or rule provides an answer.

I propose the following general rule: *a right-holder has an epistemic right when it is legally and/or morally permissible to enforce an epistemic duty.* Note that this rule applies specifically to claim-rights. This rule gives us a way of determining who, in particular, has an epistemic claim-right to what. In order to substantiate and apply this rule, it can be broken down. First, I will establish what an epistemic duty is. Second, I will establish what it means to enforce an epistemic duty. Once these are established, the question becomes one of determining when it is legally and/or morally permissible to enforce an epistemic duty. As will become clear, answering this question is often a difficult and complex task.

Before proceeding, it is worth emphasising the central role that this rule assigns to the allocation of epistemic duties. Duties are integral to the analysis of rights. In particular, directed duties – duties owed to a particular right-holder – are the necessary counterpart of Hohfeldian claim-rights. They are, as Cruft (2013) says, "at the heart of rights" (p.201). This correlation extends beyond the analysis of claim-rights to their allocation. One cannot determine the allocation of epistemic claim-rights without determining the relevant duty-bearers. In other words, one cannot determine when it is legally and/or morally permissible to enforce an epistemic duty without identifying the individual or institution that must discharge the duty, if required.

O'Neill (2005) emphasises the significance of this tight correlation between rights and duties and argues that this poses a particular challenge for advocates of universal human rights to good and services, such as food and healthcare. These rights differ from more traditional human rights such as rights to freedom and security, which are often classed as liberty rights. In the case of liberty rights, both rights and duties are universal: all of us have liberty rights and all of us have a duty towards others to respect them. By contrast, rights to things like food and healthcare reflect an asymmetry. All of us have these rights (if they are indeed universal human rights) but we do not all bear the correlative duties. I do not have a duty to test you for diabetes and you do not have a duty to cook me dinner. Crucially, as O'Neill (2005) stresses, "we cannot tell who violates a right to goods or services unless obligations have been allocated" (p.428).[21]

This is true of epistemic rights, including those expressed as universal human rights. The right to education, for example, is asserted in Article 26 of the *International Bill of Human Rights* (1948). Accordingly, all of us have the right to education. But we do not all bear the correlative duty to educate. You do not have a duty to teach me algebra any more than I have a duty to teach my next-door neighbour epistemology. Such duties, where they arise, must be allocated to particular individuals. As O'Neill (2005) puts it "rights must have well-specified counterpart obligations" (p.430). All epistemic claim-rights correlate with epistemic duties. Consequently, the allocation of epistemic claim-rights is tied to the allocation of epistemic duties.

What are epistemic duties?

What, then, is an epistemic duty? Given the centrality of epistemic duties for the analysis and allocation of epistemic rights, a detailed exposition is certainly warranted. Unfortunately, there is no space for such an exposition here. I will, to some extent, assume a sufficiently robust common understanding of the notion of duty and stipulate that an epistemic duty is a duty that concerns epistemic goods. This

---

21 O'Neill prefers the term obligation to duty. For the purposes of this book, I treat the terms obligation and duty as synonymous.

account of epistemic duty mirrors the account of epistemic rights: in its simplest form, the latter says that an epistemic right is a right concerning epistemic goods. We saw what makes a right an epistemic right in Chapter 1. The same can be said of what makes a duty an epistemic duty. Epistemic duties are duties that concern epistemic goods.

While there is not space for detailed exposition, one can add substance to the notion of an epistemic duty by looking at different types of epistemic duty. I draw inspiration for a basic taxonomy of epistemic duties from Article 19 of the *UN Declaration of Human Rights* (1948):

> Everyone has the right to freedom of opinion and expression; this right includes freedom to hold opinions without interference and to seek, receive and impart information and ideas through any media and regardless of frontiers.
>
> (*UN Declaration of Human Rights*, 1948, Article 19)

Article 19 is typically cited as that concerning freedom of expression, which, of course, it is. The article, however, covers more than a person's right to the free expression of ideas and opinions. It also highlights a person's rights to *seek*, *receive* and *impart* information. These epistemic rights correlate with a basic taxonomy of epistemic duties: duties to seek, receive and impart information.

I call this a basic taxonomy because it provides only a basic frame for the construction of a more complex and complete taxonomy of epistemic duties. It is, nonetheless, the frame around which that taxonomy can be built and so is useful for present purposes. Indeed, this basic taxonomy of three epistemic duties can be immediately doubled to six by noticing that they each comprise both a positive and a negative duty. The positive duties to seek, receive and impart information and the negative duties *not to* seek, *not to* receive and *not to* impart information.

One can see this taxonomy at work in the case of my right to know my blood sugar levels after being tested for diabetes by my doctor. In this case, my doctor has a duty to seek (collect, acquire, find out) the test results – perhaps by performing the test herself, or by getting the results from the person who did. If the latter, she also has a duty to receive (hear, listen, accept) the test results as reported to her by the person who did the test. Lastly, she has a duty to impart (tell, give, explain) the test results to me. Furthermore, she has the negative duties not to, for example, seek out irrelevant personal information about me, receive irrelevant personal information about me, or impart irrelevant personal information about someone else to me. These are the six basic types of epistemic duties. I return to this basic taxonomy in Chapter 3.

Before moving on, it is worth locating this account of epistemic duty in relation to a prominent debate in contemporary epistemology concerning doxastic responsibility, in order to differentiate it from the notion of epistemic duty that is employed there (Clifford, 1879; Feldman, 1988; Chisholm, 1991; Montmarquet, 1992; Haack, 1997; Ginet, 2001; Russell, 2001; Steup, 2001; Levy, 2007). The doxastic responsibility debate revolves around the question of what it means to be responsible for one's beliefs. In fact, much of the debate concerns the question of whether or not it is possible to be responsible for one's beliefs, particularly in such a way as to be blameworthy.

Am I responsible for my belief that the sky is blue, for example? If so, put in the terms of the debate, one might say that I have an epistemic duty to believe that the sky is blue, when it is. A duty, in other words, to believe according to the evidence (Clifford, 1879). On the other hand, if I am not responsible for my belief that the sky is blue because, say, such a belief is not under my voluntary control, one might think that I have no corresponding epistemic duty. Alternatively, one might say that I have a duty to *try to* believe according to the evidence (Chisholm, 1977). In each case, if I believe that the sky is not blue, when it is, one may ask whether I can or should be blamed for believing falsely.

The debate concerning doxastic responsibility is related to the right to believe literature encountered in Chapter 1 (on the connection see, for example, Alston (1988) and Dretske (2000)). I said there that epistemic rights, as I construe them, differ from the conception of epistemic rights found in the right to believe literature. Moreover, these are not two competing accounts of the same thing but are better characterised as two discussions employing the same terminology. A similar thing can be said of the notion of epistemic duty employed in the doxastic responsibility literature in contrast to the one that I am concerned with in this book.

Perhaps most tellingly, rights (epistemic or otherwise) do not feature centrally in the doxastic responsibility debate. As such, epistemic duties are not construed as the correlates of epistemic rights. Rather, they are discussed and analysed independently of the concept of rights and sometimes in relation to a different concept altogether. Hall and Johnson (1998), for example, assert "where there are goals, there are correlative duties" (p.129). For these authors, epistemic duties are the correlates of goals, not rights. More generally, the doxastic responsibility debate does not assign a significant (or any) role to the consideration of rights in relation to duties. This marks a notable difference from the present discussion, given the tight correlation between rights and duties in the Hohfeldian schema, particularly between claim-rights and directed duties. Epistemic duties, as they are construed in the doxastic responsibility debate, are not correlated with rights and they are not directed, they are not owed to right-holders.

In addition, in the doxastic responsibility debate, epistemic duties are not moral duties, indeed, they are to be contrasted with moral duties (Russell, 2001; Feldman, 2005). Hall and Johnson (1998), for example, state "we don't intend any moral over-tones in this use of the word 'duty'" (p.129). Nor are epistemic duties legal duties, in this debate. This is because the doxastic responsibility debate is concerned with when and what it means for a person to have a duty to form (or not form) a belief from the purely 'epistemic point-of-view'. This might mean from the perspective of rationality or rational agency, or from the perspective of some internal standards within the epistemic domain. However one characterises the epistemic point-of-view, this is a different perspective from the one I am concerned with. Epistemic rights and epistemic duties, as I construe them, are also legal and/or moral rights and duties. They form a distinct and unified class because they are rights and duties concerning epistemic goods, but they are importantly positioned within the legal and moral domains, with legal and moral work to do.

This classification of epistemic duties as legal and/or moral duties contrasts and, in some cases, conflicts with the notion of epistemic duty employed in the doxastic responsibility debate. Feldman (2005), for example, acknowledges that there are "numerous cases in which there are moral obligations to gather evidence, form beliefs, and act accordingly" (p.381). But, he says:

> in these cases the duty to gather evidence does not result from any general intellectual requirement to know things or to believe truths. They result from specific moral requirements for action ... one might say that these duties are epistemological duties simply because they are duties related to belief formation [however] ... in the familiar cases just discussed in which there are duties to gather evidence, the duties in question are moral or prudential duties, not epistemological duties.
>
> (Feldman, 2005, p.381)

Feldman (2005) explicitly denies that epistemic duties can be moral or prudential duties. According to this picture, they are fundamentally different types of things. This is not a conclusion that I aim to directly refute. There is one sense in which epistemic duties are different, in kind, to other types of duties. The point to make here is that this is the sense that is intended in the doxastic responsibility debate. There is a different and legitimate (contra Feldman) sense in which epistemic duties are rightly construed as legal and/or moral duties: the sense in which they are duties concerning epistemic goods. This is the sense I am interested in.

Again, these are not two competing accounts of the same thing but are better characterised as two discussions employing the same terminology. That is not to say, however, that these discussions cannot intersect. They surely do, in interesting ways. If, for example, it is necessary for my doctor to form a true belief about my blood sugar levels in order for her to inform me of them, then we might say that she has a duty to form a true belief about my blood sugar levels. This latter epistemic duty should not, I think, be viewed from the purely epistemic point-of-view; it is not her duty as a rational agent but her duty as a doctor. However, the extent to which her duty as a doctor requires her to be a reliable rational agent is salient. This gives rise to a host of interesting questions that connect epistemic duties, as I construe them, with epistemic duties as they are construed in the doxastic responsibility debate and leaves interesting work to be done in contemporary epistemology. For now, I have provided an account of epistemic duties: epistemic duties are duties that concern epistemic goods. They include the basic duties to seek, receive and impart information, plus the negation of each.

Enforcing epistemic duties

I now return to the question of rights allocation and to the second focal question of the chapter: who does have epistemic rights? Recall that I am answering this question with a general rule: a right-holder has an epistemic right when it is legally and/or morally permissible to enforce an epistemic duty. An epistemic duty is a duty that concerns epistemic goods. What, then, does it mean to enforce an epistemic duty and when is it legally and/or morally permissible to do so? These are the questions to be addressed in order to substantiate and apply the general rule.

In relation to the first question, a relatively straightforward answer can be given. To enforce an epistemic duty is to demand from someone that they do their epistemic duty and to hold them accountable if they do not. Such accountability may take a variety of forms including legal action, social and moral sanctions and public or private blame. Enforcement is an important element of the relationship between rights and duties. As Cruft (2013) contends, "any violable right held by some being is constituted by an enforceable directed duty owed to that being" (pp.201–202). Likewise, Wenar (2013) includes an 'appropriate enforceability' condition in his account of claim-rights (p.209). Cruft (2013) highlights the significance of this condition succinctly:

> enforceability … distinguishes directed duties we call rights from those we do not. If I help you cross the road then you owe me a duty of gratitude, but we do not call this a right. This is because enforcement of your duty to thank me is morally inappropriate.
>
> (Cruft, 2013, p.209)

This gets to the crucial point about enforcement in relation to epistemic rights and duties (and rights and duties, in general); it must be legally and/or morally permissible. The question is thus one of determining when it is legally and/or morally permissible to enforce an epistemic duty.

The answer to this question is threefold. Firstly, some epistemic rights are already recognised and protected by the law. In these cases, it is legally permissible to enforce an epistemic duty. As such, epistemic rights are directly protected by the law. Secondly, in more complex cases, the law fails to recognise epistemic rights explicitly, but protects them indirectly. In these cases, it may be morally permissible to enforce an epistemic duty but only legally permissible via some non-epistemic legislation. As such, epistemic rights are indirectly protected by the law. Thirdly, in more complex cases still, it is morally permissible to enforce an epistemic duty, even though the correlative epistemic right is not protected, either directly or indirectly, by the law. In other words, it is morally but not legally permissible to enforce an epistemic duty. The hardest of this third set are borderline cases in which it is unclear whether or not it is even morally permissible to enforce an epistemic duty.

Each of these entails a different way of applying the general rule for the allocation of epistemic rights. Moreover, these correspond to three levels of protection: (1) direct legal protection, (2) indirect legal protection and (3) moral (but not legal) protection. These levels of protection are determined by the manner in which the relevant epistemic duty can be enforced: the enforcement of epistemic duties correlates with the protection of epistemic rights. It will be useful to explore this further in order to see how the general rule for the allocation of epistemic rights corresponds to their protection. As well as filling out an answer to the current question, this will serve as a precursor for an in-depth examination of the relationship in Chapter 3.

Take the first and most straightforward set of cases in which epistemic rights are already recognised and protected by the law. These cases involve direct legal protection. Epistemic rights are directly protected by the law when epistemic goods are the explicit target of legislation. It is, for example, illegal in the UK for private individuals to listen to other people's phone calls via a warrantless tapping device, according to the Regulation of Investigatory Powers Act 2000 (RIPA).[22] Further protection regarding the acquisition and use of information comes from the UK's Data Protection Act 2018, which currently supplements the EU's General Data Protection Regulation (GDPR).[23] Consequently, if someone has placed a warrantless tapping device on my phone, I can take them to civil court and sue for breach of privacy, while the Crown Prosecution Service is responsible for prosecuting the offence itself. In other words, it is legally permissible for me (and the Crown Prosecution Service) to enforce another person's epistemic duty not to listen to my phone calls via a warrantless tapping device. As such, it is my epistemic right that other's refrain from doing so and I am directly protected in this right by the law.

Next, take the second set of cases in which epistemic rights are protected indirectly by the law. I call this indirect legal protection because, in these cases, epistemic rights are protected in virtue of legislation that targets something non-epistemic, in contrast to cases where the protection of epistemic rights is the explicit target of legislation, such as phone tapping. Epistemic rights are protected indirectly when they fall under or are subsumed by some other legal protection. It is, for example, illegal in the UK to repeatedly follow someone in public in such a way that causes them fear of violence or serious alarm or distress, according to the Protection of Freedoms Act 2012 (PFA).[24] This behaviour is classified as stalking. In addition to causing fear, alarm and distress, stalking may involve the perpetrator having access to personal information about the victim, such as their home and work addresses and contact details. Possessing such information is not in itself an offence under normal circumstances. However, protecting a victim from stalking may involve ensuring that such information is not available to a perpetrator. As such, legislation designed to protect a victim's non-epistemic rights may require protecting their epistemic rights.

In these cases, it is legally permissible to enforce another person's non-epistemic duty not to engage in stalking. Doing so also makes it

---

22 http://www.legislation.gov.uk/ukpga/2000/23/part/I [Accessed: 7 May 2020].
23 The latter is due to be incorporated directly in UK law following the UK's exit from the European Union.
24 http://www.legislation.gov.uk/ukpga/2012/9/contents/enacted [Accessed: 7 May 2020].

permissible (in certain cases) to enforce their epistemic duty not to acquire particular information about the victim. As such, the victim of stalking has epistemic rights. Their epistemic rights are not directly protected by the law but are subsumed by the more general protection against stalking provided by the PFA. Their epistemic rights are indirectly protected by the law.

Lastly, take the third set of cases in which epistemic rights are not recognised or protected by the law. The question of whether or not a person has an epistemic right in these cases must be determined by some non-legal consideration. In particular, whether or not it is morally permissible to enforce an epistemic duty.[25] This is decidedly more complex terrain. The previous case illustrates this complexity. We might, for instance, think that it is right not to make acquiring personal information about someone an explicit and autonomous legal offence, even in cases of stalking. Rather, what matters from a legal perspective is what a person does with the information, once acquired. If they use it to repeatedly follow someone to and from work, causing serious distress, they should be prosecuted. If they file it away in a draw, they should not.

However, at least plausibly, acquiring the information itself could be *morally* wrong, even if it is only filed away in a draw. Knowing that a particular person has access to their home and work addresses could be a source of serious distress to a victim. Consequently, it might still be permissible to hold a person accountable for some *moral* wrong, even when they have not done anything illegal. More generally, morality and the law diverge. We hold people morally accountable for legal actions and omissions through mechanisms such as social sanctions and blame. The question concerning the third set of cases is what makes it permissible to do so. When is it morally (but not legally) permissible to enforce an epistemic duty? Given the added complexity of these cases, I will examine them further.

We gain an insight into these cases by looking at *transactional* and *relational* rights. Hart (1955) identifies such rights, which "arise out of special transactions between individuals or out of some special

---

25 Note that there are cases in which rights and duties are established by some non-legal institution, such as a workplace or via customs and conventions. I take it that in all such cases of non-legal institutional and customary rights, a person has a right only when it is *morally* permissible to enforce a duty. Hence, all cases of rights not enforceable by law are identified by the moral permissibility of enforcing the correlative duty.

relationship in which they stand to each other" (p.183).[26] These include, for example, rights conferred by the actions of promising or consenting, as well as rights established by relationships such as parent and child, patient and doctor, or teacher and student. In the absence of any legal basis for the enforcement of duties, these transactional and relational rights provide bases for determining the moral permissibility of enforcing of duties.

It is, for example, morally permissible for you to demand that I make you a cup of tea, if I have promised you that I will. You can blame me if I fail to make the tea and tell others that I am an unreliable tea-maker. If, on the other hand, I have not promised to make you a cup of tea, it would be morally inappropriate for you to demand that I do so and to blame me if I do not. In the promising case, you have a right that I make you a tea; in the no-promising case, you do not. The same is true for epistemic goods. If I promise to tell you when I will be home, then it is morally permissible for you demand that I do so and blame me if I do not. Based on my promising, you have a right to know (or more precisely, a right that I tell you) when I will be home.

Likewise, relationships provide a basis for determining the moral permissibility of enforcing epistemic (and other) duties. We might think that a mother has the right to know when her teenage son will be home, even if he doesn't make any promise to tell her. It would be morally permissible for her to demand that he tell her when he will be home and to hold him to account, if he does not. This moral permissibility is based on their relationship as mother and son, rather than on any explicit promise or consent. It (at least sometimes) establishes her right to know when her son will be home. The same moral permissibility may hold between any primary caregiver and the individuals for whom they are responsible. It does not hold outside of these relationships. I cannot (usually) demand to know when a complete stranger's son will be home. Relationships provide a basis for determining the moral permissibility of enforcing epistemic (and other) duties.

Relational rights explain why I have a right to know my blood sugar levels after being tested for diabetes and you do not. In this context, I stand in the relevant relationship with my doctor, as her patient. As a result of this relationship, it is morally permissible for me to enforce

---

26 Hart (1955) calls these 'special rights'. However, the term 'special rights' also has a different politicised meaning in relation to civil rights movements (Marcosson, 1995; Goldberg-Hiller and Milner, 2003). To avoid confusion, I will not employ the term.

my doctor's epistemic duty to provide me with information about my blood sugar levels. I can demand that she do so and hold her to account, if she does not. It is not morally permissible for you to make the same demand or to hold her to account, if she fails. That is even if you are also her patient in another context. You are not her patient in this context because you were not the subject of this diabetes test. Transactional and relational rights provide the bases for determining the moral permissibility of enforcing duties.

In these cases, then, it is morally (but not legally) permissible to enforce an epistemic duty. As such, we can identify epistemic rights that are not protected by law. The existence of such rights, however, leads naturally to consideration of contentious or borderline cases. Without a legal basis for enforcing epistemic duties, the permissibility of such enforcement on moral grounds is inevitably less clear-cut. Imagine that your friend suspects his husband of having an affair and asks you to let him know if you see the husband behaving inappropriately around another man. You subsequently see him out to dinner with the man, holding hands and being overtly affectionate. It is clear that your friend's suspicions are well-founded. Does he have a right to know what you have seen and do you have a duty to tell him? It seems there is at least a colloquial sense in which he has a right to know. You might, for instance, justify telling him on the basis that he has a right to know if his husband is having an affair. Indeed, you might appeal to this even if your friend has never expressed any suspicions about his husband. How should we understand this colloquial appeal to the right to know?

This scenario represents a borderline case for the allocation of epistemic rights. It is one on which, I suspect, intuitions will diverge. Following the general rule in this case, we can ask whether it would be morally permissible for your friend to demand that you tell him what you have seen and for him to hold you to account, if you do not. To my mind, it is intuitively plausible that such a demand would be morally permissible only if you have promised to tell him if you see anything. Without such a promise, your relationship as friends may provide you with good reason to tell him (perhaps even a duty) but is not, I think, sufficient for establishing a right on his part. As Cruft (2013) puts it in the case of helping someone to cross the road, absent the promise, enforcement of your duty would be morally inappropriate. However, intuitions in borderline cases such as this are likely to diverge. It is important to acknowledge that such cases exist and are inevitable, given the complex moral terrain on which we all must tread.

There is more to be said about transactional and relational epistemic rights. Which transactions and which relationships, in particular, serve as the basis for enforcing epistemic duties? There is not space to cover this complex ground here and, consequently, these important questions must be left for future work. That said, the preceding discussion has highlighted the significance of the enforceability of epistemic duties for the allocation of epistemic rights. It is this that gives weight and value to the general rule for allocating epistemic rights. As such, the general rule provides an answer to the second focal question: a right-holder has an epistemic right when it is legally and/or morally permissible to enforce an epistemic duty. In conjunction with the answer to the first focal question, this concludes the investigation into who has epistemic rights.

Summary

In this chapter, I have answered two focal questions: who can have epistemic rights and who does have epistemic rights? In answer to the first, I have argued that all right-holders qualify as epistemic right-holders, including (at least) all presently existing humans. In answer to the second, I have argued that a particular epistemic right-holder has a particular epistemic right when it is legally and/or morally permissible to enforce an epistemic duty. Such enforcement is determined either directly or indirectly by the law, or on moral grounds through the existence of transactional and relational rights. These two answers serve as a combined response to the title question of the chapter: who has epistemic rights? As such, they provide the basic conceptual resources for determining who has epistemic rights.

The existence of contentious and borderline cases regarding the allocation of epistemic rights nonetheless demonstrates the complexity of the challenge embarked upon in this chapter, as do whistle-blowing cases, such as that of Snowden. These cases reflect a complex matrix of epistemic rights and epistemic duties, positioned against a background of intricate legal decision-making and moral intuitions. The questions these (and other less contentious) cases give rise to matter because they relate directly to the level of protection that those involved, including the public at large, can and should expect from both society and the law. If we do not have good answers to these questions, then we risk leaving those who require protection exposed to harm due to the violation of their epistemic rights. In Chapter 3, I turn to an examination of epistemic rights violations and protections, detailing further cases and emphasising the practical significance of the questions that have been addressed in Chapters 1 and 2.

3   When are epistemic rights violated?

Epistemic rights feature in many diverse domains of contemporary life. I have so far introduced two cases that illustrate this: Purdue Pharma and Edward Snowden. Despite obvious differences in terms of context, subject matter and so on, both cases raise important and pressing questions concerning epistemic rights. Significantly, these cases do not merely illustrate the nature of epistemic rights and their role in our everyday lives. They also provide an insight into what happens when epistemic rights 'go wrong'. In other words, they are cases in which epistemic rights are violated.

In this chapter, I examine the nature and extent of epistemic rights violations, drawing on the Purdue Pharma and Snowden cases, as well as several new ones. These provide a context in which to examine epistemic rights violations and demonstrate the scope of such violations across every arena of our lives. Where there are epistemic goods – information, knowledge truth – there is the possibility of its mistreatment. Where we have rights concerning epistemic goods, there is the possibility that their mistreatment constitutes a violation of our rights. In general, the cases I discuss are those in which I believe epistemic rights violations have occurred. Inevitably, some of these may be contentious and certainly all of them are open to further debate. The purpose of this chapter is not to argue for definitive answers to the question of when (and whether) epistemic rights have been violated in particular, real-world cases. The purpose is to raise the question and show why it is a useful and important question to ask.

I noted in the introduction that most discussions of rights distinguish between two questions: the question of what a right is (or what it means to have a right) and the question of what rights we have. The first question is more explicitly analytical while the second is more political. The analytical work of Chapters 1 and 2 has sharpened the lens regarding epistemic rights. Such a lens magnifies and clarifies, allowing us to see epistemic rights in operation in a range of real-world scenarios where they might otherwise be obscured. This clarity is vital for a proper appreciation of the nature and extent of epistemic rights violations in the twenty-first century. With this theoretical grounding in place, I now approach the political question, and task, in more concrete terms. I do so by asking three focal questions. Firstly, what epistemic rights violations are there? Secondly, what protections are in place for epistemic rights? Thirdly, are these protections sufficient? Before addressing these focal questions, I will elucidate what it means for an epistemic right to be violated.

What does it mean for an epistemic right to be violated?

Epistemic rights, as with most, if not all other rights, can be violated. A right is violated when any duties resulting from that right, to perform, or not to perform certain actions, are unjustifiably disregarded. This is what it means for a right to be violated. By way of elucidation, one can contrast rights violations with rights infringements (Gewirth, 1981). A person's right is infringed when actions required by that right are not performed, or actions prohibited by that right are performed.

My right to use my mobile phone is infringed if you seize it off me and throw it in the river. However, infringing a person's right does not necessarily amount to violating their right. If I am about to call emergency services to falsely report a bomb threat in a public park, then you have good reason to seize my mobile phone and throw it in the river. This constitutes a justifiable infringement of my right. A person's right is violated when it is *unjustifiably infringed*. In other words, when actions required by that right are unjustifiably not performed, or actions prohibited by that right are unjustifiably performed. If I am about to call a mutual friend to ask if she would like to meet us in the park, then (let's assume) you have no good reason to seize my mobile phone and throw it in the river. This would constitute an unjustifiable infringement, and thereby a violation, of my right.

The same is true for epistemic rights. An epistemic right is violated when any epistemic duties resulting from that right, to perform, or not to perform certain actions, are unjustifiably disregarded. I have a right to know my blood sugar levels after being tested for diabetes. If my doctor misinforms me about them, then she is infringing my right. If she does so with no good reason (and it is hard to imagine what a sufficiently good reason would be), then she unjustifiably infringes, and so violates, my right.

The question of whether a right (epistemic or otherwise) has been violated, therefore, rests on the question of whether the duty-bearer is *justified* in disregarding the correlative duties. This question is naturally a source of both legal and moral disagreement. Snowden, for example, believed that the secrecy of the NSA's surveillance activities was an unjustifiable infringement of the public's right to know about widespread surveillance. If this judgement is correct, then the secrecy of the surveillance constituted a violation of the public's right to know. Others, including Barack Obama, have argued that this infringement was justified, for reasons of national security.[27] If that judgement is correct, then the secrecy of the NSA programmes constituted an infringement, but not a violation, of the public's right to know. As such, in this case and many others, much depends on the question of whether an infringement can be justified. While this is a vital question for determining how we should respond in any particular case, it is not the question I am addressing in this chapter. As noted, I will assume that all the cases discussed involve at least some genuine violations, as opposed to mere infringements.

One's epistemic rights can be violated in numerous ways. In order to appreciate the full scope of epistemic rights violations, it is worth once again emphasising the significance of the relationship between rights and duties. I am focusing centrally on epistemic claim-rights with correlative epistemic duties. A claim-right not only picks out a claim to protection on behalf of the right-holder but, at the same time, imposes a duty on another party towards the right-holder with respect to that claim. Claim-rights are violated when such duties are unjustifiably disregarded. This is why characterising epistemic rights in terms of the full Hohfeldian schema, and focusing on claim-rights, is significant. Doing so allows us to identify certain actions and omissions concerning epistemic goods *as violations*. That one's epistemic rights can be violated is a central claim. Again, an epistemic right is violated when any epistemic duties resulting from that right, to perform, or not to perform certain actions, are unjustifiably disregarded.

What epistemic rights violations are there?

There are numerous forms of epistemic rights violations. These correspond to unjustifiable disregard for numerous forms of epistemic duties. I offered a basic taxonomy of epistemic duties in Chapter 2 and return to this now to identify different forms of epistemic rights

27 https://www.theguardian.com/world/2013/dec/20/obama-snowden-leaks-caused-unnecessary-damage [Accessed: 18 May 2020].

violations. The basic taxonomy included six epistemic duties: the positive duties to seek, receive and impart information and the negative duties not to seek, not to receive and not to impart information.[28] Epistemic rights are violated when duties to perform or not perform one or another of these acts are unjustifiably disregarded. What does this look like in the world around us? It will be useful here to return to the Purdue Pharma case to illustrate some of the most prevalent epistemic rights violations. Each of these violations corresponds to disregard for one (or more) of the basic epistemic duties.

Recall that in 2007, Purdue Frederick Company Inc., along with its president, chief legal officer and chief medical officer, were charged with criminal misbranding of the opioid OxyContin, after admitting that the drug was marketed "with the intent to defraud or mislead."[29] Purdue consistently and systematically distorted information about OxyContin, including with respect to its effectiveness, abusability and addictive properties. As such, the company and its executives unjustifiably disregarded their epistemic duties and, in doing so, violated their customers' epistemic rights. Several prominent forms of epistemic rights violations are illustrated in this case.

Firstly, Purdue knowingly propagated falsehoods about the safety profile of OxyContin in order to convince medical professionals that it was safer than other opioids on the market. For example, they instructed sales representatives to tell doctors that the risk of addiction from the drug is less than 1% when in fact it is much higher. As Paul Hanly, a lawyer who attempted to bring a criminal trial against Purdue in 2003, stated "These pronouncements about how safe the drug was emanated from the marketing department, not the scientific department... They just made this stuff up."[30] Purdue knowingly propagated falsehoods regarding the safety profile of OxyContin and, in doing so, unjustifiably disregarded their epistemic duty. This duty correlates with the epistemic rights of their customers to accurate information about the safety profile of OxyContin. As such, Purdue violated their customers' epistemic rights. The *propagation of falsehoods* is a common form of epistemic rights violation.

---

28 Recall that this taxonomy was inspired by Article 19 of the *UN Declaration of Human Rights* (1948) in which the language 'seek, receive and impart' is used. Beyond this, nothing much is meant to hang on this choice of words. They each have a number of synonyms that can be substituted but I see no reason to do that here.

29 https://www.newyorker.com/magazine/2017/10/30/the-family-that-built-an-empire-of-pain# [Accessed 26 Nov 2019]

30 https://www.newyorker.com/magazine/2017/10/30/the-family-that-built-an-empire-of-pain# [Accessed 26 Nov 2019]

Secondly, as well as propagating outright falsehoods, Purdue engaged in extensive misinformation regarding various aspects of OxyContin. For example, a key original selling point of OxyContin over other opioids was the time-release formula that allowed patients to take the painkiller every twelve hours, rather than every eight, making dosages easier to adhere to. However, Purdue was aware that not all patients would respond to the time-release formula in the same way. An early study of OxyContin users in Puerto Rico showed that approximately half of the patients taking the drug required further doses before twelve hours.[31] Three *LA Times* journalists behind a 2016 exposé highlighted the damage caused by improper dosage:

> OxyContin is a chemical cousin of heroin, and when it doesn't last, patients can experience excruciating symptoms of withdrawal, including an intense craving for the drug.[32]

Nonetheless, Purdue pushed the twelve-hour time-release formula as a key selling-point in its marketing of OxyContin, misleading both doctors and patients into believing that two doses at twelve-hour intervals would be effective for all. Purdue knowingly propagated misinformation about the effectiveness of a key element of OxyContin. In doing so, as before, they unjustifiably disregarded their epistemic duty and so violated their customers' epistemic rights. The *propagation of misinformation* is another common form of epistemic rights violation.

Thirdly, the propagation of misinformation often relies heavily on a policy of withholding information. This has the effect of distorting one's assessment of the misinformation that is made available. Purdue knowingly withheld vital information regarding the risks and effectiveness of OxyContin from the outset. For example, the study of Puerto Rican patients that found the twelve-hour time-release formula to be ineffective for half of patients, was never published. Later evidence that also demonstrated this, as well as complaints from prescribing doctors, were similarly ignored and supressed.[33] As *New Yorker* journalist Patrick Radden Keefe comments:

> For Purdue, the business reason for obscuring such results was clear: the claim of twelve-hour relief was an invaluable marketing

---

31 https://www.latimes.com/projects/oxycontin-part1/ [Accessed: 20 May 2020]
32 https://www.latimes.com/projects/oxycontin-part1/ [Accessed: 20 May 2020].
33 https://www.latimes.com/projects/oxycontin-part1/ [Accessed: 20 May 2020].

tool. But prescribing a pill on a twelve-hour schedule when, for many patients, it works for only eight is a recipe for withdrawal, addiction, and abuse.[34]

Purdue knowingly *withheld information* about the effectiveness of OxyContin's time-release formula. Again, this amounts to an unjustifiable disregard of their epistemic duty and represents another common form of epistemic rights violation.

In addition to propagating false and misleading information, and withholding accurate information, Purdue also unjustifiably disregarded their duty to receive information about OxyContin's time-release formula from the authors of the Puerto Rican study. In other words, they failed to take the results of the study seriously and act accordingly. In fact, Purdue failed to take seriously the results of multiple further studies and warnings from numerous other key individuals and organisations, including the FDA as well as, according to 2007 US Attorney General John Brownlee, "health care professionals, the media, and members of its own sales force that OxyContin was being widely abused and causing harm".[35]

Moreover, despite clear evidence from multiple studies that OxyContin is required at shorter than twelve-hour intervals for many patients, Purdue failed to run any studies testing the effectiveness of OxyContin at shorter intervals, such as the standard eight-hour intervals required for many other painkillers. Doing so would have undermined their competitive advantage. By failing to conduct such studies, Purdue unjustifiably disregarded their epistemic duty to seek vital information about the safety profile and addictive properties of OxyContin. Purdue's unjustifiable disregard for their epistemic duties both to receive and to seek vital information about OxyContin amount to further violations of their customers' epistemic rights.

A final, widespread form of epistemic rights violation is also worth highlighting. I call this the *abuse of perceived epistemic authority*. Abuse of perceived epistemic authority is possible in any situation where an individual or organisation is perceived as an epistemic authority on a given subject. In other words, where they are perceived as a source of accurate, reliable and relevant information about that subject.

---

34 https://www.newyorker.com/magazine/2017/10/30/the-family-that-built-an-empire-of-pain# [Accessed 20 May 2020].
35 https://www.health.mil/Reference-Center/Publications/2007/05/10/The-Purdue-Frederick-Company-Inc-and-Top-Executives-Plead-Guilty [Accessed 6 Feb 2020].

Crucially, abuse of perceived epistemic authority is made possible by an individual or organisation's *perceived* rather than actual epistemic authority (so regardless of whether they in fact are an authority on a given subject). As a major global producer of pharmaceuticals, Purdue Pharma can reasonably be perceived as a source of accurate, reliable and relevant information about its own pharmaceutical products. Particularly if one has no knowledge of, for example, the misinformation practices that they have systematically employed. A doctor who is not aware of these practices and is told by a Purdue salesperson that OxyContin has an effective twelve-hour time-release formula and a risk of addiction at less than 1% might, reasonably and blamelessly, form the corresponding false beliefs and prescribe OxyContin on this basis. Her patients, moreover, being one step further removed, might well perceive the doctor as an epistemic authority on which drugs they should take to relieve pain. As a result, a patient might, reasonably and blamelessly, inherit her doctor's false beliefs regarding OxyContin and/or act on the basis of them.

The abuse of perceived epistemic authority is particularly pernicious when overt epistemic power-dynamics are in play. A person is more likely to believe information on a given subject when it comes from a source that they perceive to be an epistemic authority, especially if they have good reason for doing so. This can lead to credibility excess, whereby unwarranted credibility is given to information from a perceived epistemic authority, even though it is in fact false or misleading (Fricker, 2007; Medina, 2011). Doctors and patients at the sharp end of Purdue's manipulative and misleading sales, and marketing practices are not only at risk of receiving false, misleading and incomplete information about OxyContin, they are also at risk of assigning unwarranted credibility to that information as a result of the abuse of perceived epistemic authority. This constitutes a widespread and pernicious form of epistemic rights violation.

In summary, the epistemic rights violations in play in the Purdue Pharma case include, at least, propagating false or misleading information, withholding accurate information, failing to collect, take seriously and publicise relevant, vital information, and abusing perceived epistemic authority. These by no means represent all possible forms of epistemic rights violation. They are, however, some of the most prevalent and significant. Other examples of these, as well as other forms of epistemic rights violations, will become apparent in due course. All epistemic rights violations can be understood in terms of the basic taxonomy of epistemic duties: duties to seek, receive and impart information, plus the negation of each. This taxonomy indicates what epistemic rights violations there are and, as in the case of Purdue Pharma, what they look like in the world around us. Having thus addressed the first focal question of the chapter, I will move to the second.

What epistemic rights protections are in place?

In Chapter 2, I argued that in order to determine who has epistemic rights, we must ask when it is legally and/or morally permissible to enforce epistemic duties. Such enforcement is determined either directly or indirectly by the law, or on moral grounds through the existence of transactional and relational rights. These different modes correspond to three different levels of protection for epistemic rights: (1) direct legal protection, (2) indirect legal protection and (3) moral (but not legal) protection. To recap, epistemic rights are directly protected by the law when epistemic goods are the explicit target of legislation. Epistemic rights are indirectly protected by the law when epistemic goods are not the explicit target of legislation, but are protected as a result of legislation because they fall under or are subsumed by some other legal protection. Epistemic rights are morally (but not legally) protected when they can be established on moral grounds but are not protected, either directly or indirectly, by the law.

Epistemic rights are directly protected by many thousands of individual laws including freedom of information laws, data protection and privacy laws, libel and slander laws, marketing and advertising laws, intellectual property laws and many others. Epistemic rights are indirectly protected by criminal laws, banking and finance laws, corporate laws, commercial and consumer laws, tax laws, family laws and many others. Epistemic rights are morally (but not legally) protected by moral and social sanctions, such as public protest, public or private pressure, and public or private blame. It is not hard to find plentiful examples of the latter in the current political climate. One need only pick up a newspaper or turn to the various social media platforms to find accusations of lies, deceit, fake news, and 'truth-twisting'.[36] In short, epistemic rights are protected in many different ways and these protections range widely across the law and across different aspects of our lives and communities.

36 https://www.forbes.com/sites/carltonreid/2020/05/24/civil-service-tweet-goes-viral-arrogant-and-offensive-can-you-imagine-having-to-work-with-these-truth-twisters/#16cc09c63154 [Accessed: 26 May 2020].

Direct legal, indirect legal and moral protections constitute three levels of protection for epistemic rights. In essence, this provides an answer to the second focal question. However, a closer look at these levels of protection, as they manifest in real-world cases, will help to further substantiate that answer. From the outset, it is worth noting that even in cases where epistemic rights have direct or indirect legal protection, it is not the case that the term 'epistemic rights' is being used in the law. In fact, I am not aware of the term epistemic rights being used in any legal settings, including those centrally involving rights concerning epistemic goods. Thus, when I say that epistemic rights are directly or indirectly protected by the law, I simply mean that those rights that I call epistemic rights are directly or indirectly protected by the law.

Notably, however, the phrase 'right to know' does arise in a variety of legal settings. It is, for instance, used, particularly in the US, to designate a set of environmental laws concerning exposure to dangerous or harmful chemicals in workplaces and communities. These 'worker's right to know' laws mandate, for example, that toxic substances in the workplace must be disclosed to employees. These laws were prompted by the work of public health officials, beginning in the 1950s, attempting to draw public attention to an "age of abject victimization amid manufactured ignorance" in relation to occupational health risks (Derickson, 2016, p.237). They constitute direct legal protection of epistemic rights.

A second set of US laws, often referred to as 'women's right to know' laws, are laws concerning the information that a woman must be exposed to if she is considering an abortion. These laws mandate, for example, that a woman must be told about at least one of the following: the (purported) link between abortion and breast cancer, the (purported) ability of a foetus to feel pain and the (purported) negative mental health consequences of abortion. Several states, such as Texas and Oklahoma, also require that a woman seeking an abortion be given a sonogram allowing her to hear the heartbeat of the foetus, if possible.[37, 38] These right to know laws feature centrally in the heated US abortion debate. From a pro-choice perspective, women's right to know laws arguably violate women's epistemic rights while, from a pro-life perspective, these laws represent direct legal protection of epistemic rights (see Watson (2020) for a more detailed discussion).

A third set of laws sometimes referred to as right to know laws, particularly in a European context, are laws concerning a child's right to

---

37 https://dshs.texas.gov/wrtk/ [Accessed: 26 Feb 2019].
38 https://www.awomansright.org/ [Accessed: 27 May 2020].

know. Article 7 of the *Convention of the Rights of the Child* (1989) states that a child has "as far as possible, the right to know and be cared for by his or her parents" (p.7). These right to know laws emerged in separate European countries from the 1980s onwards and were recognised internationally in 1989 in both the *Convention of the Rights of the Child* and in corresponding amendments to the *European Convention of Human Rights*. A child's right to know her biological origins is now recognised as a human right by states party to these conventions. These laws again constitute direct legal protection of epistemic rights.

Worker's, women's and child's right to know laws all take epistemic goods as the explicit target of legislation. A less clear-cut example, in terms of the three levels of protection, comes from consideration of victim's right to know laws. Specifically, a set of international criminal justice laws concerning the victims of mass atrocities and human rights violations. These laws have been negotiated over several decades since the end of the Second World War and are now ratified by numerous international bodies, including the *General Assembly of the United Nations* and the *Inter-American Court of Human Rights* (Ferrer Mac-Gregor, 2016). These laws aim to protect the families of deceased or missing victims of mass atrocities and those having themselves experienced such atrocities. The UN, for example, affirms:

> the importance of determining the truth with regard to crimes against humanity, genocide, war crimes and gross violations of human rights" and "the right of the families to know about the fate of their sick, wounded and deceased relatives, and ... the importance of the truth in transitional justice.
>
> (Ferrer Mac-Gregor, 2016, p.132)

These laws explicitly identify the 'right to know the truth' or 'the right to know what happened' as a central feature of justice for victims in the wake of mass atrocities and human rights violations.

However, this right is not always recognised as an autonomous right. In some cases, for example involving the forced disappearance of persons, it has been subsumed under more general rights to procedural justice (Ferrer Mac-Gregor, 2016). In these cases, the right to know is indirectly, rather than directly protected. Judge Ferrer Mac-Gregor (2016) has nonetheless argued that the law should recognise and treat these rights as autonomous and inalienable:

> Court case law can evolve in such a way that strengthens the full recognition of the right to know the truth, acknowledges the

autonomy of this right, and establishes its content, meaning and scope with increased precision.

(Ferrer Mac-Gregor, 2016, pp.125–6)

Victims' right to know laws thus represent a complex set of laws that either directly or indirectly protect epistemic rights, depending on interpretation of the law. The question of which level of protection is appropriate concerns the precise nature and relative import of epistemic rights.

Similar complexity arises when considering right to know laws in the context of private, interpersonal relationships. One might think that such cases should be excluded from legal consideration altogether. In other words, that there are no legally enforceable private rights to know. The law should not, for example, determine what we can demand to know about our lovers, friends and family, even if it is morally permissible to make such demands, in certain cases. However, consider a case in which a person engages in unprotected sexual intercourse without revealing to their sexual partner that they have a serious sexually transmitted infection, such as HIV. In California, in 2015, a man was found guilty of intentionally infecting another person with HIV and sentenced to six months in prison and a $1000 fine. The city attorney at the time, Jan Goldsmith, said in a local radio interview:

> I hope this case helps to educate people that it is a crime to wilfully expose someone to an infectious disease... The law is designed to protect the public and, in this case, the right of one's partner to know the truth.[39]

In this case, the epistemic rights of the relevant party were not only indirectly, but directly protected by the law. Indeed, Judge Katherine Lewis called for the offense to be upgraded to a felony, stating that her inability to give out a harsher sentence constituted "a tremendous oversight in the law".[40] Rather than dismissing the idea of a legally enforceable private right to know, according to Judge Lewis, there is cause for greater direct legal protection.

---

39 https://www.advocate.com/hiv/2015/3/11/san-diego-man-pleads-guilty-spreading-hiv [Accessed: 25 May 2020].

40 https://www.washingtonpost.com/news/morning-mix/wp/2015/05/05/man-who-knowingly-spread-hiv-sentenced-to-six-months-judge-calls-it-a-travesty/ [Accessed: 25 May 2020].

Laws vary widely across the world with respect to these cases. In the UK, individuals who have knowingly exposed others to HIV without disclosing it have been prosecuted for grievous bodily harm (GBH).[41] In these cases, a person's epistemic rights are indirectly protected by the law. Physical harm caused by transmission of HIV is the explicit target of the legislation but one's right to know is indirectly protected because ignorance intersects with one's ability to consent to a known risk of infection. If one knows about the risk and consents to unprotected sex, the charge of GBH is not applicable, even if the infection is transmitted. As such, the difference between knowing and not knowing has significant legal and moral consequences, determining, in some cases, whether or not a crime has been committed at all, even one as serious as GBH. As with victim's right to know laws, the question of which level of protection is appropriate concerns the precise nature and relative import of epistemic rights.

A final example concerns the 'public's right to know'. This notion is often invoked in order to inspire moral sanctions such as public protest and blaming practices. As such, cases involving the public's right to know typically (but not always) concern moral rather than legal protection of epistemic rights.[42] Perhaps the most familiar invocation of the public's right to know appears in relation to freedom of the press. This is often attributed to the former Executive Director of the *Associated Press* in New York, Kent Cooper, who argued passionately, in *The Right to Know: An Exposition of the Evils of News Suppression and Propaganda* (1956), for freedom of the press as a means of ensuring the public's right to impartial information about world events, urging that the right to know must be viewed as a public, rather than private good.

Just three years earlier, legal scholar and journalism specialist, Harold L. Cross had also published his influential book, *The People's Right to Know: Legal Access to Public Records and Proceedings* (1953), regarded by many as the original source for the modern language

---

41 http://www.e-lawresources.co.uk/R-v-Dica.php [Accessed: May 26 2020].

42 There is much to be said about the nature of 'the public' as an entity capable of having rights, and the nature of groups as epistemic agents, more generally (see Mathieson, 2006; Lackey, 2014; David, 2020). One may view groups either as wholly reducible to their individual members or as epistemic entities in their own right. I assume that intuitive sense can be made of the notion of the public's right to know without resolving this interesting epistemological debate, so will remain neutral regarding this.

surrounding freedom of information (Cuillier, 2016). Cross opened with the words:

> Public business is the public's business. The people have a right to know. Freedom of information is their just heritage. Without that the citizens of a democracy have but changed their kings.
>
> (Cross, 1953, p.1)

The work of media professionals and legal specialists, such as Cooper and Cross, has enshrined the public's (or people's) right to know as a core principle of press freedom, freedom of information and, indeed, of democracy itself. In the US, the notion has become somewhat synonymous with the First Amendment of the US Constitution. Both Cooper (1956) and Cross (1953), in fact, argued for a constitutional amendment that would restate the First Amendment in terms of the people's right to know, as opposed to freedom of speech or the press. Issues concerning the public's epistemic rights run deep in the contours of contemporary democracy.[43]

The case of Snowden and the leaked NSA documents provides a clear example. In a 2014 interview with German public radio and television broadcaster NDR, Snowden was asked about his motivations for blowing the whistle on the NSA programmes. He said:

> The public had a right to know about these programs. The public had a right to know that which the government is doing in its name, and that which the government is doing against the public, but neither of these things we were allowed to discuss, we were allowed no, even the wider body of our elected representatives were prohibited from knowing or discussing these programmes and that's a dangerous thing.[44]

Snowden's actions brought the notion of the public's right to know in cases of government surveillance to the fore in international debate. Later

---

43 Despite its wide uptake as a cornerstone of press freedom, the notion of the public's right to know also has its critics. Journalism scholar Blanchard (1986), for example, criticised Cooper and others for a post-war 'First Amendment crusade', outside of the US. Following the Second World War, attempts to enshrine the public's right to know in international settings were met with resistance, for example in Russia and much of Europe, based on the concern that 'American style' freedom of information would facilitate abuses, rather than liberation, of the press (Cifrino, 1989).

44 https://edwardsnowden.com/2014/01/27/video-ard-interview-with-edward-snowden/ [Accessed: 28 May 2020].

that same year, the public's right to know was formally articulated in the *Tshwane Principles on National Security and the Right to Information* (2013). Principle 10E states that "The public has a right to know about systems of surveillance, and the procedures for authorizing them" (p.2). Principle 4 identifies the relevant duty-bearer: "It is up to the government to prove the necessity of restrictions on the right to information" (p.1).

The *Tshwane Principles* were developed collaboratively between twenty-two organisations and institutions, based on international and regional laws and standards.[45] They are not laws themselves but rather guidelines. As such, they do not provide any legal protection of the public's right to know about systems of global surveillance. As in cases related to press freedom, protection of the public's right to know often relies on moral, rather than legal sanctions (including the act of whistleblowing itself). Thus, the public's right to know often falls under the third type of protection for epistemic rights, namely, moral (but not legal) protection.

There is, of course, much more that can be said on all of these topics. For now, the examples have helped to fill out an answer to the second focal question of the chapter, illustrating different levels of protection that exist for epistemic rights: direct legal protection, indirect legal protection, and moral (but not legal) protection. The examples also illustrate the strikingly different domains of public and private life to which these protections pertain. Moreover, they provide a rich context for the third focal question of the chapter: are these protections sufficient?

Are epistemic rights protections sufficient?

For any type of protection, one can ask whether that protection is doing its job. Does it actually protect the thing that it is meant to protect? One can ask whether it is the right type of protection, for example legal or moral, and whether it is the right degree of protection: should whatever we are trying to protect be more or less protected? If it is the case that a different type of protection offers a different degree of protection, then these questions are interrelated. Both type and degree of protection are relevant when asking whether epistemic rights protections are sufficient.

Each level of protection for epistemic rights gives rise to a specific version of this question. First, in cases where epistemic rights are directly protected by the law, one can ask whether these rights should be *better* protected by the law. Second, in cases where epistemic rights are indirectly

---

45 https://www.right2info.org/exceptions-to-access/national-security/global-principles [Accessed: 28 May 2020].

protected by the law, one can ask whether these rights should be *directly* protected by the law. Third, in cases where epistemic rights are not protected by the law, one can ask whether these rights should be protected *by the law*. These questions cover extensive and complex legal and moral ground; it is not my aim to answer them here for any particular case.

Nonetheless, the examples in the previous section demonstrate the diverse contemporary contexts in which these questions can be asked. One can ask, for example, if the direct legal protections provided by workers' right to know laws do enough to protect workers from the occupational health risks posed by the use of novel chemicals and toxins in the workplace. One can ask whether women's right to know laws in the US abortion debate in fact go too far and violate, rather than protect women's epistemic rights. One can ask, along with Judge Ferrer Mac-Gregor (2016), if victims' right to know laws should provide direct protection for the epistemic rights of families and victims, rather than subsuming these rights under more general legal protections. And one can ask whether there should be legal, rather than exclusively moral protection of the public's right to know, for example, in cases of widespread misinformation in the media or government directed systems of global surveillance. These questions are just some of the many that arise when one begins to shine a critical light on the protections that are currently in place for epistemic rights.

In order to answer the third focal question, I will focus on the three questions above as they pertain to the central case of Purdue Pharma. As a result of the 2007 trial and Purdue's admission that OxyContin was marketed "with the intent to defraud or mislead",[46] the company and three of its top executives were ordered to pay fines totalling $634 million. This ruling represents direct legal protection of epistemic rights. It explicitly targets epistemic goods and establishes a legal basis for enforcing Purdue's epistemic duties with respect to those goods, picking out particular duty-bearers and holding them accountable, through criminal charges and fines. These epistemic duties correlate with the epistemic rights of Purdue's customers, both doctors and patients, including the right to have accurate information about the effectiveness, abusability and addictive properties of OxyContin.

The high-profile case and $634 million fine represent direct legal protection of epistemic rights. There are, however, a number of reasons to ask whether these rights can and should be *better* protected by the law.

---

46 https://www.newyorker.com/magazine/2017/10/30/the-family-that-built-an-empire-of-pain# [Accessed 26 Nov 2019].

Firstly, those commenting on Purdue's misleading marketing and manipulative sales strategies note that these techniques had been entrenched within the company for almost 50 years (Meier, 2019). This indicates an extensive heritage of institutionalised epistemic rights violations not accounted for in the 2007 trial.

Secondly, while the trial identified Purdue's top executives as duty-bearers, it is clear that they are not the only ones responsible for epistemic rights violations relating to the sale and marketing of OxyContin. Plausibly, a large number of individuals employed by Purdue, and perhaps some of its key prescribing doctors, have not been held directly accountable for epistemic rights violations.

Thirdly, one can ask whether the legal penalty accurately reflects the seriousness of the harms caused by these epistemic rights violations. US Attorney John Brownlee stated that, following Purdue's "fraudulent marketing campaign ... scores died as a result of OxyContin abuse and an even greater number of people became addicted to OxyContin."[47] One can legitimately question whether a $634 million fine (or indeed any fine) represents an appropriate penalty in response to this kind of devastation. Indeed, Republican senator for Pennsylvania, Arlen Specter commented, after the 2007 Purdue trial, that fines such as this amount to no more than "expensive licenses for criminal misconduct".[48] One can thus question not only the appropriateness but also the effectiveness of fines for preventing future epistemic rights violations. These fines represent a legal basis for holding pharmaceutical giants to account for epistemic rights violations but there is reason to question whether the laws that prescribe them go far enough. Should epistemic rights that are directly protected by the law, be better protected by the law?

One can also ask whether epistemic rights that are indirectly protected by the law, should be directly protected by the law in the Purdue Pharma case. An area in which epistemic rights are often indirectly, rather than directly protected by the law is healthcare. In the Purdue Pharma case, it is possible that some of the highest prescribing doctors were aware of the addictive properties of OxyContin and continued to prescribe it, nonetheless. This of course violates numerous professional codes, including the primary maxim in the healthcare profession to 'do no harm'. Doctors can be held legally accountable for such actions.

---

47 https://www.health.mil/Reference-Center/Publications/2007/05/10/The-Purdue-Frederick-Company-Inc-and-Top-Executives-Plead-Guilty [Accessed 6 Feb 2020].
48 https://www.newyorker.com/magazine/2017/10/30/the-family-that-built-an-empire-of-pain# [Accessed 26 Nov 2019].

In Missouri in 2017, for example, a doctor and his employer, St Louis Hospital, were found guilty of medical malpractice for overprescribing opioids, and ordered to pay $17.6 million in damages.[49]

Misinforming or lying to patients about the addictive properties of OxyContin would form part of the cause for action in a case such as this, as well as constituting evidence of malpractice. However, an epistemic rights violation would not typically suffice, in its own right, for prosecution. In other words, the mere fact that a doctor lies to a patient about OxyContin in order to, say, take advantage of a large bonus offered by Purdue Pharma, would not typically be sufficient to hold her legally accountable for medical malpractice, unless a (further) harm is caused. A doctor's epistemic duties are thus subsumed under a more general duty of care which is, in turn, understood in terms of physical (and increasingly psychological) but not necessarily epistemic harms. The epistemic rights of OxyContin patients are thus often only indirectly protected by the law.

Should these rights be directly protected by the law? There are a number of reasons for thinking that they should. Firstly, the practice of lying to or deliberately misinforming patients, especially if it is widespread or pernicious, is likely to erode trust in the patient-doctor relationship and in the medical profession at large. Trust is widely recognised as a key component of successful healthcare, at both the individual and societal level, and a lack of trust in the healthcare profession could have devastating consequences for patients and doctors alike. Secondly, dishonest practices, such as lying and misleading, reflect bad professional character and plausibly correlate with diminished levels of individual accountability. Thirdly, lying to or deliberately misinforming a patient is, in some cases, arguably itself a damaging form of disrespect, which represents a harm in its own right. I explicate these harms, and others, in Chapter 4. They are vital for considering the question of when and whether epistemic rights that are indirectly protected by the law, should be directly protected by the law.

Lastly, one can ask if epistemic rights that are not protected by the law, should be. While three of the top executives at Purdue Pharma have been charged and fined in relation to epistemic rights violations, there have so far been no legal repercussions for any individual members of the Sackler family that owns the company. The Sacklers have, however, profited substantially from sales of OxyContin and many of the deceptive

49 https://www.paulsonandnace.com/can-doctor-held-liable-patients-opioid-abuse-17-6-million-verdict-says-yes/ [Accessed: 2 June 2020].

and aggressive strategies that characterise its marketing are attributed to the leadership of Arthur Sackler in the 1970s (Meier, 2018). It is plausible that members of the Sackler family are responsible, either directly or indirectly, for epistemic rights violations in the Purdue Pharma case. Despite the lack of any apparent legal accountability for the Sacklers, the family have nonetheless been held morally accountable, through social and political action, by those who believe that they bear some responsibility for the ongoing opioid crisis. In 2017, the artist Nan Goldin founded an advocacy organisation, P.A.I.N. (Prescription Addiction Intervention Now). The organisation has targeted the Sackler family through its website – sacklerpain.org – as well as public protests in the US, the UK and France, held at art galleries, museums and universities where they have made philanthropic donations and are often recognised with named galleries, wings and institutes.[50] Banners at these protests read "Take down the Sackler name" and protesters chant "Shame on Sackler."[51]

Public protests, blame and shame, are key forms of moral protection for epistemic rights violations. As well as being bad PR, such protests can contribute to other less public sanctions. Following a P.A.I.N. protest in London, the National Portrait Gallery became the first major gallery to drop plans for a Sackler grant, a move that was noted as "a landmark victory in the battle over the ethics of arts funding" in subsequent media coverage.[52]

Moreover, the media itself has a role to play in accurately representing the opioid crisis, communicating with the public and placing companies such as Purdue Pharma and the Sackler family in the limelight, to ensure accountability. If and when the media fails to do so, it is also at risk of violating the epistemic rights of its audience: the public right to know. In fact, the media has played an important role in investigating and exposing the harms caused by OxyContin and the part played by Purdue Pharma in the opioid crisis. The popular and influential John Oliver Show ran a feature on this, for example.[53] Media coverage and investigative journalism are critical forms of moral protection

50 https://www.bloomberg.com/news/articles/2019-03-06/sackler-family-faces-art-world-protests-with-purdue-under-siege [Accessed: 2 June 2020].

51 https://www.theguardian.com/world/2019/jul/01/nan-goldin-protests-against-sackler-wing-at-the-louvre [Accessed: 2 June 2020].

52 https://www.theguardian.com/world/2019/jul/01/nan-goldin-protests-against-sackler-wing-at-the-louvre [Accessed: 2 June 2020].

53 https://www.theguardian.com/culture/2019/apr/15/john-oliver-hires-actors-to-unbury-sackler-deposition-on-opioids-crisis?ref=hvper.com [Accessed: 15 Dec 2020].

for epistemic rights. Both media attention and public protest, however, often arise because of a lack of direct or indirect legal protection against harm and injustice. This is true in cases concerning epistemic rights, such as the Purdue Pharma case. As such, they require us to ask if epistemic rights that are not protected, either directly or indirectly, by the law, should be protected by the law.

This investigation of the Purdue Pharma case in relation to the question(s) of epistemic rights protections offers an illustration of the complex legal and moral issues brought about by the third and final focal question of the chapter. Many of these issues require us to consult intricate moral intuitions that have not been validated by existing legal rulings. Despite these challenges, and in fact, because of them, the question(s) of whether or not the current protections that exist for epistemic rights, across diverse domains of public and private life, are sufficient, is both relevant and, in some cases, pressing. Answering these questions requires further rigorous debate and attention to individual cases. The investigation in this chapter has, nonetheless, provided an insight into the nature and extent of epistemic rights violations in contemporary life.

Summary

In this chapter, I have examined epistemic rights violations through three focal questions: what epistemic rights violations are there? What protections are in place for epistemic rights? And, are these protections sufficient? I have drawn on the central case of Purdue Pharma to illustrate several prominent types of epistemic rights violations and an underlying taxonomy structured around the six basic epistemic duties: to seek, receive and impart information, plus the negation of each. In addition, I have introduced a suite of further examples, exploring different contexts for epistemic rights violations and protections. I have identified three levels of protection for epistemic rights: (1) direct legal protection, (2) indirect legal protection and (3) moral (but not legal) protection. These three levels are associated with different versions of the third focal question concerning whether or not protections for epistemic rights are sufficient. In Chapter 4, I highlight the significance of the topics explored here by investigating and categorising the harms caused by epistemic rights violations.

4 Who gets hurt?

Epistemic rights violations cause harm. By now this point may appear obvious or simplistic and in some sense it is. It is nonetheless an important, if not critical point to make and to emphasise. Indeed, it is perhaps the key point of the book. Epistemic rights violations harm our lives, our relationships, our social and political institutions and our communities. The significance of this cannot, in my view, be overstated. The cases discussed so far provide context for a discussion of the harms caused by epistemic rights violations. In addition, I will introduce one final case that underlines this point.[54]

According to UNAIDS, the global organisation primarily tasked with tackling the HIV/AIDS pandemic, AIDS is estimated to have caused 32 million deaths worldwide since it was first identified in the early 1980s (as of 2018).[55] The propagation of false and misleading information about HIV and AIDS have accompanied the pandemic from the outset (Boer and Emons, 2004; Kalichman, 2009; Weller, Webber and Levy, 2017). Misinformation ranges over almost all facets of the disease and is cited by both scholars and healthcare professionals as an important factor, which continues to exacerbate its spread and prevents those infected from getting diagnosed and accessing treatment (Boer and Emons, 2004; Kalichman, 2009, 2014; Nattrass

---

54 The fact that epistemic rights violations cause harm is not the only reason to be concerned about them. This consequentialist framing supplies a useful and, I think, powerful mechanism for articulating the significance of epistemic rights violations. However, a deontological or virtue-based reading of epistemic rights violations may also be appropriate and add richness to the overall picture. There is not space to develop these readings here but it is important to note that I do not intend to be exclusivist about the appropriate normative theory for interpreting the wrong of epistemic rights violations.
55 https://www.unaids.org/en/resources/fact-sheet [Accessed: 16 Jan 2020].

and Kalichman, 2009; Chigwedere and Essex, 2010; Fourie and Meyer, 2011; Weller, Webber and Levy, 2017).

A catastrophic example of the propagation of false and misleading information concerning HIV and AIDS has come to be known as AIDS-denialism (Kalichman, 2009, 2014; Nattrass and Kalichman, 2009; Fourie and Meyer, 2011). AIDS-denialism is the belief that HIV is not the cause of AIDS. Two prominent versions of this view exist. The more widespread centres on the belief that HIV is a harmless passenger virus which plays no causal role in AIDS; a view propagated by the discredited molecular biologist, Peter Duesberg (Nattrass, 2010). AIDS-denialists of this stripe attribute the cause of AIDS to behavioural factors such as sexual behaviour and recreational drug use, environmental factors such as malnutrition and poor sanitation, or biological factors such as haemophilia. In addition, following Duesberg, some claim that antiretroviral drugs – the drugs developed to delay the progression of HIV to AIDS – in fact cause AIDS (Duesberg, Koehnlein and Rasnick, 2003).

AIDS-denialists exist in all corners of the world. However, AIDS-denialism has had an especially damaging effect in South Africa, largely due to a sustained period of government endorsement and propagation of misinformation concerning HIV and AIDS during the 2000s, led by the former South African president Thabo Mbeki and former Health Minister Manto Tshabalala-Msimang (Kalichman, 2009; Chigwedere and Essex, 2010). Initially, Mbeki questioned the safety of the antiretroviral drug zidovudine (AZT) for pregnant women, claiming that legal cases concerning the drug were underway in the US and the UK and that he had received "dire warnings" about the drug's toxicity.[56] As reported in an article in *The Lancet* at the time (1999) "Glaxo Wellcome, the manufacturers of the drug, said Mbeki appeared to have been "gravely misinformed"" and confirmed that there was "no legal action on its safety pending anywhere".[57] The misinformation that Mbeki appealed to came largely from the website virusmyth.com, as well as from Duesberg, whom Mbeki employed the following year as part of an investigative commission into the disease (Chigwedere and Essex, 2010).

On the basis of this misinformation, Mbeki withdrew government support from clinics that had begun using AZT to treat HIV-infected

---

56 https://www.thelancet.com/journals/lancet/article/PIIS0140-6736(05)76703-9/fulltext [Accessed: 17 Jan 2020].

57 https://www.thelancet.com/journals/lancet/article/PIIS0140-6736(05)76703-9/fulltext [Accessed: 17 Jan 2020].

pregnant women. Following this, government policies on the use of antiretrovirals in South Africa became increasingly restrictive, including restricting the use of Nevirapine, an antiretroviral donated by the pharmaceutical company Boehringer Ingelheim in 2000, and the delayed implementation of a national antiretroviral treatment plan. Mbeki also obstructed the acquisition of grants for AIDS treatment from the Global Fund (Chigwedere and Essex, 2010, p.237).

Overwhelming scientific consensus confirms that HIV causes AIDS (O'Brien and Goedert, 1996; Essex and Mboup, 2002; Robert, Gallo, and Luc Montagnier, 2003; Chigwedere and Essex, 2010). Chigwedere and Essex (2010) offer a succinct account of the evidence:

> HIV meets several standards of epidemiologic causality. HIV has satisfied Koch's postulates, the traditional standard of infectious disease causation... Using a causal model developed for chronic disease, HIV satisfies all of Sir Bradford Hill's guidelines for assessing causality... [including identification of] an almost *unique* pathophysiological mechanism of how HIV leads to AIDS through the loss of CD4 lymphocytes.
> (Chigwedere and Essex, 2010, p.238, emphasis original)

In other words, outside of AIDS-denialism circles, there is no doubt within the international scientific and political community that HIV causes AIDS. Significant progress in prevention and treatment of the disease has been made in the last several decades on this basis.

The effects of AIDS-denialism in South Africa have been devastating. Chigwedere et al. (2008) estimate that "at least 330,000 South Africans died prematurely and 35,000 babies were infected with HIV as a result of Mbeki's policies" (p.237) between 2000 and 2005. These shocking figures are at the higher end of those attested to by others in the scientific community but the key point behind the analysis is beyond dispute, as Nattrass (2010) confirms:

> the fact that deaths and new HIV infections could have been averted had antiretrovirals been used sooner, is incontrovertible. Chigwedere and Essex are correct to emphasize this, and to point out, once again, that there is no scientific basis for AIDS denialism.
> (Nattrass, 2010, p.250)

In the case of AIDS-denialism in South Africa, the harms caused by widespread and pernicious epistemic rights violations have amounted to devastation of arguably genocidal proportions.

The aim of this chapter is to characterise and catalogue the harms caused by epistemic rights violations, such as those found in the case of South African AIDS-denialism. Who and what gets hurt as a result of these violations? There is just one focal question of the chapter, reflected in the chapter title. A more precise expression of this question will help to make the target clear: what harms are caused by epistemic rights violations? I will answer this question in several stages, drawing on cases that have been presented throughout the book. In doing so, I seek to underline the ongoing, real and significant threat that epistemic rights violations pose.

Epistemic rights violations and epistemic injustice

Before answering the focal question directly, it will be useful to examine the notion of epistemic injustice. Many important epistemic harms have been brought to attention in contemporary epistemology and beyond, through Miranda Fricker's seminal exposition of this notion in *Epistemic Injustice: Power and the Ethics of Knowing* (2007). This has provided a lens through which to view the sometimes harmful effects of the epistemic dimension of our lives, and a vocabulary with which to articulate these. Notably, Fricker does not speak of epistemic rights. The relationship between rights and justice is, however, a close one, as much in the epistemic domain as any other. In order to characterise the harms caused by epistemic rights violations it will, therefore, be useful to explicate the relationship between epistemic rights violations and epistemic injustice.

Fricker highlights two forms of epistemic injustice, which she terms testimonial injustice and hermeneutical injustice. Testimonial injustice concerns the amount of credibility that is assigned to a speaker in a testimonial exchange. One can assign too much credibility (credibility excess) or too little (credibility deficit). In essence, this amounts to how much one believes what another person says. Testimonial injustice occurs when hearers assign too little credibility to speakers on the basis of identity prejudicial stereotypes. This happens when something a person says is not believed because they are, for instance, black or a woman.

Hermeneutical injustice concerns the conceptual resources and vocabulary available to members of a community. This form of epistemic injustice occurs when members of a community lack the conceptual resources and vocabulary to make sense of and articulate their situation, including common feelings and experiences. Fricker uses the case of sexual harassment to illustrate hermeneutical injustice. Before the concept of sexual harassment was widely available, those experiencing it were unable to adequately make sense of and articulate experiences of sexual harassment. As such, they suffered from collective hermeneutical injustice. As Fricker (2007) demonstrates, both testimonial and hermeneutical injustice result in significant harms.

It is useful, I think, to conceive of epistemic justice and injustice as a function of epistemic rights. By this I mean that, when epistemic rights are respected, epistemic justice will typically prevail. Conversely, when epistemic rights are violated, epistemic injustice will typically be the result. Thus, epistemic justice typically involves respect for epistemic rights and epistemic injustice typically involves the violation of epistemic rights. I say typically because, while the relationship between rights and justice is a close one, it is not one of conceptual necessity. In other words, rights can be violated without the occurrence of injustice and injustice can occur without the violation of rights. Nonetheless, epistemic rights violations can often be identified in cases of epistemic injustice.

In cases of testimonial injustice, for instance, the hearer's duty to give due credit to the speaker in testimonial exchange is unjustifiably disregarded. Thus, the speaker's epistemic right to be believed without prejudice is violated. In cases of hermeneutical injustice, a complex set of duties attaches to groups and institutions within a community, correlated with the epistemic rights of its members to share in the practices that determine meaning for the community. Hermeneutical injustice often arises when such duties are unjustifiably disregarded and the associated epistemic rights are violated. Both these forms of epistemic injustice typically involve the violation of epistemic rights.

Other forms of epistemic injustice do too. Coady (2010) highlights a form of epistemic injustice arising from the unfair distribution of epistemic goods, such as information and education. He argues that this kind of distributive injustice constitutes a distinctive and important form of epistemic injustice. Coady refers to this kind of distributive epistemic injustice as "unjust ignorance or error" (p.110). As with testimonial and hermeneutical injustice, distributive epistemic injustice is typically connected to epistemic rights violations. In these cases, a person's right to know is disregarded, either because they are ignorant about something that they are entitled to know, or because they are wrong about something they are entitled to be right about (Coady, 2010, p.109). Coady argues that both the forms of epistemic injustice identified by Fricker and distributive injustice are "widespread forms of injustice, which, when systematic, as they often are, constitute a form of oppression that afflicts those with relatively little social power" (p.110). These oppressive injustices involve the violation of epistemic rights.

By way of illustration, we can see all these forms of epistemic injustice in the case of AIDS-denialism in South Africa. The voices and suffering of marginalised and vulnerable groups were not taken seriously (testimonial injustice), while the voices of a few privileged individuals, such as Duesberg, were given excess credibility. The ability to make sense of and articulate the experience of AIDS was diminished by widespread misinformation about its nature and cause, and the associated stigma that accompanied these (hermeneutical injustice). Access to accurate information and education about HIV and AIDS was heavily restricted and, where available, unfairly distributed, favouring those able to receive a formal education in the first place, with access to resources such as the internet (distributive injustice). The epistemic rights violations that feature centrally in these instances of epistemic injustice are a primary source of the many harms arising as a result. Epistemic rights violations and epistemic injustice are often closely linked.

What harms are caused by epistemic rights violations?

A wide range of harms are caused by epistemic rights violations. These harms occur at the level of individuals and communities. In reality, there is no strict dividing line between these levels. Harms done to individuals will often be reflected in their communities and harms done to communities will impact upon their individual members. Nonetheless, distinguishing between these levels of harm allows us to appreciate the way in which violations negatively impact different aspects of our social structures.

One can also draw a further distinction, employed by Fricker (2007), between primary and secondary harms. Primary harms are essential to epistemic rights violations themselves. In other words, they are what it means for an epistemic rights violation *to be a wrong.* Secondary harms are not essential to the violation itself but occur as a further harmful consequence. Fricker (2007) draws this distinction when discussing the harms caused by epistemic injustice. She says of primary harm that it is "a form of the essential harm that is definitive of epistemic injustice" (p.44) while secondary harm is "composed of a range of possible follow-on disadvantages, extrinsic to the primary injustice in that they are caused by it rather than being a proper part of it" (p.46). I draw on this distinction to characterise and catalogue the harms caused by epistemic rights violations.[58]

---

58 It is worth noting that not all harms in the epistemic domain are caused by epistemic rights violations. Moreover, there may be something distinctive about harms that are caused by rights violations, including epistemic rights violations, such that they are worse, in some sense, than, for example, harms caused by rights infringements. There is not space to address this here but it represents one of many important questions raised by the consideration of epistemic rights as a substantive form of rights.

Primary harm: Epistemic injury

In her discussion of the harms caused by epistemic injustice, Fricker (2007) notes:

> There is of course a purely epistemic harm done when prejudicial stereotypes distort credibility judgements: knowledge that would be passed on to a hearer is not received. This is an epistemic disadvantage to the individual hearer, and a moment of dysfunction in the overall epistemic practice or system.
>
> (Fricker, 2007, p.43)

This 'purely epistemic harm' is also one of the primary harms caused by epistemic rights violations. When a person's right to information or knowledge is violated, say because they have been lied to or misinformed, they are put at an epistemic disadvantage that reflects dysfunction in the epistemic system. I call this *epistemic injury*. Note that epistemic injury (like any injury) can occur without violating a person's epistemic rights; the cause of the injury may be an accident, in which no epistemic duties are unjustifiably disregarded. An epistemic rights violation, however, cannot occur without either actual or attempted epistemic injury; the injury is an essential feature of the violation. This is what makes it a primary harm. I will explicate this harm by returning, once again, to the Purdue Pharma case.

In 1996, an early, widely circulated press release for OxyContin emphasised the efficacy and positive benefits of the opioid's 12-hour time release formula:

> Unlike short-acting pain medications, which must be taken every 3–6 hours – often on an "as needed" basis – OxyContin tablets are taken every 12 hours, providing smooth and sustained pain control all day and all night.
>
> (1996, p.1)

The press release continued with testimony from the then Vice President of Purdue Pharma, Paul D. Goldenheim, M.D.: "The importance of pain control with twice daily dosing can't be stressed strongly enough" (1996, p.1). Many journalists and doctors who saw the press release, and those who read subsequent press coverage based on it, came to believe that OxyContin could (and indeed should) be taken safely at 12 hour intervals. However, as noted, as many as half those taking OxyContin require additional medication before 12 hours in order for the drug to provide effective pain relief and to avoid withdrawal symptoms. Consequently, those who came to falsely believe the press release were put at an epistemic disadvantage by being deprived of accurate information about the drug.

The epistemic disadvantage for the person who believes that OxyContin can and should be taken safely at 12-hour intervals comes from the deprivation of epistemic goods. Simply put, this person knows less, has a poorer understanding and is less well-informed about the drug, than the person who believes a true statement concerning OxyContin, for example, that many people need to take OxyContin more regularly on an 'as-needed' basis. They are also, plausibly, at an epistemic disadvantage to a person who has not seen the press release and has no beliefs about OxyContin's time-release formula. This is because the press release not only deprives a person of epistemic goods but also provides them with 'epistemic bads' or 'bad epistemic goods'. Just as a person who is given a rotten apple is at a nutritional disadvantage to a person who is given a good apple, they are also at a disadvantage to a person who has no apple. Eating a rotten apple will have negative effects for the digestive system that a person with no apple will not suffer.

In the case of beliefs about OxyContin, the person who believes that the drug has an effective 12-hour time-release formula may suffer further negative effects to their epistemic system. For example, they may form the related false belief that OxyContin is better than other pain medications on the market. The person who believes truly and the person who has no beliefs about OxyContin's time-release formula will not form this further false belief. Moreover, the person who believes falsely is not only put at an epistemic disadvantage in relation to others but also when assessed according to general epistemic standards, for example, the twin goals of believing truths and avoiding falsehoods (James, 1896). The person who believes falsely is failing according to these standards.

Patients have a right to accurate information about the safety profile of OxyContin, including the efficacy of its time-release formula. Purdue Pharma have a duty to provide this information – a duty that the company unjustifiably disregarded in the 1996 press release. This constitutes an epistemic rights violation. When a person's epistemic rights are violated they are put at an epistemic disadvantage and suffer epistemic injury. As Fricker (2007) notes, this kind of harm is found in cases of testimonial injustice. Similarly, it can be identified in cases of distributive epistemic injustice in the form of "unjust ignorance or error" (Coady, 2010, p.110). Epistemic injury is a primary epistemic harm arising from epistemic rights violations.

The harm done to individuals through epistemic injury, moreover, extends to the epistemic community. A person who falsely believes that OxyContin is the best pain medication on the market because of its 12-hour time-release formula may pass this information on to others, who come to believe it too. Human beings rely on this ability to communicate information between members of their communities. If enough members of a community come to share a false belief, the community as a whole is put at an epistemic disadvantage, both when compared to other communities and when assessed according to general epistemic standards. This is epistemic injury at the level of the epistemic community.

In the case of extensive misinformation campaigns such as that orchestrated by Purdue Pharma, the epistemic community is increasingly a global one. Given this, the spread of false and misleading information through the use of a press release is particularly troubling. The goal here was clearly not to influence the beliefs of doctors and patients on an individual basis but to use extensive networks of science communication and the media to contaminate the whole epistemic ecosystem. Purdue "set out to perpetrate a fraud on the entire medical community", as lawyer Paul Hanly put it.[59]

That was in 1996. Just a quarter century later, humans can communicate faster than ever before, through a dazzling array of mediums including the many forms of social media. False and misleading information that is spread using these mediums can be picked up by hundreds of thousands of people in a matter of hours. Indeed, multiple recent studies have shown that misinformation spreads faster than truth on social media (Vosoughi, Roy and Aral, 2018; Brown, 2018). Thus, epistemic injury can be inflicted on the global community with relative ease. According to the artist Nan Goldin and her advocacy organisation P.A.I.N., the threat posed by Purdue Pharma is increasingly global too: "this crisis has killed hundreds of thousands of Americans and it's coming Europe's way. This is an emergency."[60]

In the information-centric world of the twenty-first century, the connection between individual and communal epistemic injury is arguably tighter than it has ever been. Consequently, the scale of the potential harm caused by epistemic injury is both extensive and troubling, ranging across many domains of public and private life. Purdue Pharma is

59 https://www.newyorker.com/magazine/2017/10/30/the-family-that-built-an-empire-of-pain# [Accessed: 26 Nov 2019].

60 https://www.theguardian.com/world/2019/jul/01/nan-goldin-protests-against-sackler-wing-at-the-louvre#maincontent [Accessed: 4 June 2020].

by no means an exceptional case. It nonetheless illustrates the nature of this primary harm. Epistemic injury is an epistemic disadvantage that is essential to epistemic rights violations. Epistemic rights violations cause harms that threaten the proper functioning of our individual and collective epistemic lives.

Primary harm: Epistemic Insult

Epistemic injury is not the only form of primary harm caused by epistemic rights violations. Another harm consists in the wrong done to individuals (and, thereby, communities) in their capacity as epistemic agents. I call this *epistemic insult*. Like epistemic injury, epistemic insult is a primary harm because it is essential to epistemic rights violations; it is what it means for an epistemic rights violation *to be a wrong*. One can see the distinction between these two forms of primary harm through an analogy with regular insult and injury. A person who is knocked down by a car in the street and suffers an injury is put at a physical disadvantage. If the car drives away without stopping, they also suffer an insult. The harm done by the insult does not necessarily put them at a further disadvantage but it is nonetheless a harm. This harm comes from wronging the person in their capacity as a human, a being of value deserving of due care and respect. The act of driving away adds (criminal) insult to injury.

The same is true in the epistemic case. If my doctor lies to me about the results of my blood sugar test, or deliberately misinforms me about the risks of the drugs she is prescribing, she puts me at an epistemic disadvantage. In addition to this, by lying to or deliberately misinforming me, she also insults me in my capacity as an epistemic agent. She fails to treat me with the due care and respect I am entitled to as an epistemic agent (with epistemic rights). Thus, adding epistemic insult to epistemic injury.

In some respects, the epistemic insult may be considered the greater or more fundamental harm. Carel and Kidd (2014, 2017), place a spotlight on the distinctive vulnerability of ill persons to epistemic harms resulting from epistemic injustice in the healthcare system. These harms consist not only in the epistemic (and ultimately practical) disadvantages that arise from lacking information about or being unable to understand one's own medical condition but also in "persistent experiences of feeling ignored, marginalised, or epistemically excluded by health professionals" (Carel and Kidd, 2017, p.173). The latter are forms of epistemic insult that represent a primary harm of epistemic rights violations in the domain of healthcare.

Epistemic insult is the form of harm that Fricker (2007) is centrally concerned with in *Epistemic Injustice*. She speaks of the person who suffers epistemic injustice as being "wronged in her capacity as a knower" (p.44) and says of this primary harm, "To be wronged in one's capacity as a knower is to be wronged in a capacity central to human value" (p.44). Fricker signals the significance of this harm by highlighting the key role played by the capacity for knowledge and reason in humanity's sense of its own value:

> We are so long familiar with the idea, played out by the history of philosophy in many variations, that our rationality is what lends humanity its distinctive value. No wonder, then, that being insulted, undermined, or otherwise wronged in one's capacity as a giver of knowledge is something that can cut deep. No wonder too that in contexts of oppression the powerful will be sure to undermine the powerless in just that capacity, for it provides a direct route to undermining them in their very humanity.
>
> (Fricker, 2007, p.44)

Fricker's attention at this point in the book is on the wrong of testimonial injustice. As such, she focuses on the subject of injustice as one who imparts knowledge – as a testifier. However, this is not the only sense in which a person can be harmed in her capacity as a knower (or epistemic agent). There is an important, if subtle, difference between being harmed in one's *capacity as a knower* and being harmed in one's *capacity to impart knowledge*. Most notably, one's capacity as a knower is not exhausted by one's capacity to impart knowledge. As epistemic agents, we also seek and receive knowledge from others. Wronging a person in her capacity to impart knowledge, such as in cases of testimonial injustice, can therefore be viewed as a restricted form of a more general epistemic harm. Being wronged in one's capacity as a knower includes, but is not limited to one's capacity to impart knowledge. Rather, it incorporates one's capacity to seek, receive *and* impart knowledge. As noted, this tripartite set is reflected in Article 19 of the *UN Declaration of Human Rights* (1948). The article appears to neatly represent all three fundamental aspects of a person's 'capacity as a knower'.

Wronging someone in her capacity as a knower or, as I will write from hereon, as an epistemic agent can, therefore, consist in harming her in any one of three fundamental aspects: as someone who is seeking, receiving, or imparting epistemic goods. As discussed in Chapter 3, these fundamental aspects correlate with a basic taxonomy of epistemic duties. Epistemic rights violations occur when these duties are unjustifiably disregarded. Thus, this primary epistemic harm correlates with the different ways in which epistemic rights can be violated. Whether one's rights are violated in the process of seeking, receiving or imparting epistemic goods, the harm of epistemic insult is an essential feature of this violation. Fricker is, I think, right to emphasise the deep significance of this harm.

Considering victims' rights to know in cases of mass atrocities and human rights violations brings this starkly into focus. As we saw in Chapter 3, Judge Ferrer Mac-Gregor (2016) argues that victims' rights to know should be treated as 'autonomous and inalienable' rights. He references cases of the forced disappearance of persons, judged by the *Inter-American Court*, in which victims' families have been given no official version of events concerning the disappearance of loved ones. Ferrer Mac-Gregor stresses that "uncertainty about what happened to their loved ones is one of the main causes of mental and moral suffering of the relatives of the disappeared victims" (p.138). The suggestion of 'moral suffering' captures something of the nature and force of the epistemic insult in this case and echoes the deep significance of this harm expressed by Fricker (2007). Ferrer Mac-Gregor (2016) quotes the UN High Commissioner on Human Rights, who asserts that "the truth is fundamental to the inherent dignity of the human person" (p.132). Epistemic insult is a primary and, at times, profound harm arising from epistemic rights violations.

Moreover, it is plausible that this form of harm can be inflicted on whole communities. In essence, epistemic insult concerns a lack of due care and respect. It is a form of maltreatment and this maltreatment can extend to communities. It is disrespectful for a doctor to lie to her patient about the effects of a medication she is prescribing. Likewise, it is disrespectful for a major pharmaceutical company to lie to the "entire medical community"[61] about the safety profile of its products. Rowan Cruft (2013) examines precisely this intuition: "Violation of any duty owed to a person, animal *or group* is disrespectful to that person, animal *or group*" (p.202, emphasis added). Cruft explores a number of explanations for this intuition and argues that there remains a puzzle about how to fully account for it. Nonetheless, the thought that lying to, deceiving or misinforming a person or a group are all forms of disrespect is compelling. Not only this, but they are forms of disrespect that can 'cut deep' as Fricker (2007) puts it.

---

61 https://www.newyorker.com/magazine/2017/10/30/the-family-that-built-an-empire-of-pain# [Accessed: 26 Nov 2019].

Epistemic injury and epistemic insult comprise two forms of primary harm arising from the violation of epistemic rights. These are serious harms affecting both individuals and communities across many domains. They must be taken as significant and distinctive harms in their own right in order for us to fully appreciate the nature and extent of the damage done by epistemic rights violations in contemporary life.

Secondary harm

In addition to primary harms, there are numerous secondary harms caused by epistemic rights violations. To recap, secondary harms are not essential to epistemic rights violations; epistemic rights violations can occur (and harm) without any secondary harms arising. Secondary harms constitute further or follow-on disadvantages resulting from epistemic right violations. Fricker (2007) discusses the secondary harms of epistemic injustice, distinguishing between two categories of secondary harm: the practical and the epistemic (p.46). Practical secondary harms include, for example, being convicted of a crime one didn't commit or being held back in one's career, as a result of testimonial injustice. The "(more purely) epistemic [secondary] harm" (p.47) includes, for example, losing confidence in one's beliefs or, in cases of persistent testimonial injustice, intellectual ability more generally. Fricker contends that persistent testimonial injustice can also impede the development of intellectual virtues and so impact upon "the harmony of a person's overall intellectual character" (p.50).

Again, both these forms of secondary harm arise as a result of epistemic rights violations and affect individuals and communities. Before examining these, it is worth drawing attention to Fricker's (2007) subtle qualification regarding the 'more purely' epistemic secondary harms (p.47). Fricker traverses both the epistemic and moral terrain, successfully drawing these domains together and demonstrating their interconnectedness. She speaks at some length, for example, of testimonial justice as a hybrid intellectual-ethical virtue (pp.120–128). I have followed this same path across the intellectual-ethical landscape, in particular, recognising the moral and legal significance of epistemic rights. As such, the distinction between epistemic and practical harms should be taken, as Fricker indicates, as a useful means of carving up broad types of harm, rather than as a strict demarcation. It should be clear by now that the relationship between 'the epistemic' and 'the practical' is a tight one and their influence on each other is substantial.

Secondary harm: Epistemic

The epistemic secondary harms caused by epistemic rights violations include the right-holder losing confidence in her beliefs or intellectual ability, more generally. One can think of this as a kind of downstream effect of epistemic insult and injury. Being put at an epistemic disadvantage and being wronged as an epistemic agent are harms in their own right. In addition, they may disrupt one's epistemic system by making one question one's other beliefs and/or lose confidence in one's ability to form true beliefs, or perform other cognitive tasks, in the first place.

In reference to cases of forced disappearance, Aguilera (2013) quotes Marcus Funk (a leading commentator of the International Criminal Court's framework for victim participation): "Victims seek the truth because the truth, to some extent at least, alleviates their anguish [and] vindicates their status" (p.125). This anguish is undoubtedly a deeply moral and emotional anguish but, crucially, it is caused by a violation of epistemic rights and is also an epistemic anguish. The anguish of simply not knowing. Such anguish, especially when experienced over a sustained period, may well lead victims to question their memories and beliefs about past events in an attempt to fill the gaps left by epistemically unresolved trauma. This is more likely if those in positions of power deliberately withhold, obscure or otherwise corrupt the relevant epistemic goods. As Funk asserts (quoted in Aguilera (2013)), "[Establishing the truth] makes it more difficult for those accused to create fictionalised, self-serving accounts of what occurred" (p.125). Such fictionalised, self-serving accounts constitute a particularly pernicious form of gas-lighting for the victims. The effects of this on victims' confidence in their own beliefs and experiences is a troubling form of secondary epistemic harm caused by epistemic rights violations.

Notably, the abuse of perceived epistemic authority is especially significant when considering this secondary harm. In cases of primary harm, a duty-bearer need not be in a position of perceived epistemic authority in order to violate another's epistemic rights. In contrast, secondary epistemic harm is more likely to arise from the violation of epistemic rights if the duty-bearer is in a position of perceived epistemic authority. One is more likely to question one's own beliefs if conflicting (mis)information comes from a perceived authoritative source. Certainly the abuse of perceived epistemic authority is in play when governments deliberately obscure the truth about what happened in cases of mass atrocities and human rights violations. Likewise, when a doctor intentionally misleads a patient about the safety profile and effectiveness of a drug she is prescribing. A patient may well come to question her own experiences of pain and withdrawal, before she questions her doctor's veracity.

These harms, moreover, impact upon the epistemic community. In the first place, they are likely to lead to a degradation of trust among members. In the second place, they reduce capacity for informed deliberation and debate. Again, this is especially significant in cases involving unequal power relations between community members, where perceived epistemic authority is abused. This is the case when government's withhold vital information about mass atrocities and human rights violations and when doctor's or pharmaceutical companies lie about the safety profile of drugs. What are the grounds for trust, when such violations come to light? If you know that your doctor can be convincingly misled by Big Pharma about one drug, it is not unreasonable to question her advice on any other drug, or, for that matter, the advice of any other doctor. Misinformation and deception are important factors in relations of trust and distrust. When epistemic rights violations are widespread or persistent (or perhaps just widely reported), they can quite reasonably lead to a degradation of trust between members of a community.

Widespread epistemic rights violations also reduce capacity for informed deliberation and debate within communities. If a number of individuals have been misinformed or lied to, they are, by definition, less well placed to engage in informed debate because they do not have the information in the first place. Of course, who has accurate information is often (and increasingly) a key point of contention in public debate. Epistemic rights violations that lead, for example, to 'unjust ignorance or error', make the ground on which informed debate takes place significantly less stable, or remove it altogether, for those whose rights have been violated. Epistemic rights violations reduce and undermine the capacity for informed debate within communities, especially when they are widespread, persistent and involve the abuse of perceived epistemic authority.[62]

Turning back to individuals, epistemic rights violations can also inhibit the formation of intellectual character, including the

---

62 There is significantly more to be said about the impact of epistemic rights violations on trust within communities and on their capacity to engage in informed, non-polarised debate. It is not, however, difficult to appreciate the negative impact of epistemic rights violations in these respects.

development of intellectual virtues such as curiosity, open-minded-ness, intellectual humility, intellectual courage and intellectual auton-omy (for more on the intellectual virtues, see Zagzebski, 1996; Baehr, 2011; Battaly, 2015; Watson, 2018a). Epistemic rights violations that have the effect of undermining a person's beliefs or intellectual abili-ties, may also serve to reduce her capacity for intellectual courage and/or intellectual autonomy. This is particularly true when such violations are widespread, systemic or play a central role in epistemic injustice.

The widespread violation of epistemic rights in the mainstream media provides a pertinent illustration of this secondary harm. When the mainstream media fails to serve the public's right to know by, for example, propagating false or misleading information, it can have a negative impact on the intellectual character of its audiences. A per-son who consumes the news exclusively from one or another unreliable news source, for example, is at risk of forming an extensive network of self-supporting, false beliefs, reducing her capacity for open-minded and autonomous evaluation of alternative ideas and perspectives. In addition, the systematic presentation of false or misleading informa-tion, such as when several news sources report the same falsehood, may diminish a person's capacity for intellectual humility and lead to arrogance or dogmatism. In general, widespread epistemic rights vio-lations in the mainstream media are not likely to be conducive to the cultivation of intellectual character in their audiences (Watson 2018b).

This secondary harm is especially striking when epistemic rights violations are perpetrated against large groups or entire communi-ties. Audiences of the mainstream media constitute these kinds of large groups. This is also the case with respect to exclusionary prac-tices in the delivery of education. Article 26 of the *UN Declaration of Human Rights* (1948) states that "Everyone has the right to education" (Article 26). This is one of the most extensive and fundamental epis-temic rights to be recognised and protected on the international stage. Despite this, many countries still do not have elementary education for all and exhibit significant disparities in access to education, par-ticularly between boys and girls (*Global Education Monitoring Report*, 2016). This large-scale violation of epistemic rights of course has many adverse effects, leading to significant primary and secondary harms in the epistemic and moral domains. As a barrier to the cultivation of intellectual character, it is also non-trivial.

The negative impact of exclusionary education practices on the cultivation of character was recognised and forcefully emphasised by women's rights pioneers such as Mary Astell (1694) and Mary Wollstonecraft (1792). Both were writing in Britain at a time when most women were excluded from education beyond the elementary stage (many received no elementary education either) and education, even up to this point, differed dramatically for boys and girls. Education for women was predominantly viewed as a means of instructing them in, for example, home-making, 'feminine sensibility' and etiquette (Barker-Benfield, 1992; Jones, 2006). In her then radical text, *A Vindication of the Rights of Woman* (1792), Wollstonecraft argued vehemently that women's character and their capacity for virtue was fundamentally inhibited by their exclusion from the comprehensive education received by men:

> women must be allowed to found their virtue on knowledge, which is scarcely possible unless they be educated by the same pursuits as men. For they are now made so inferior by ignorance and low desires, as not to deserve to be ranked with them; or, by the serpentine wrigglings of cunning, they mount the tree of knowledge, and only acquire sufficient to lead men astray.
>
> (Wollstonecraft, 1792, p.105)

Women, Wollstonecraft (1792) argued, were simply not given the opportunity to develop the virtues proper to all humans, regardless of sex, due to their lack of access to education. Rather, "Gentleness, docility, and a spaniel-like affection are... consistently recommended as the cardinal virtues of the sex" (p.32). As such, the widely accepted view that women were incapable of moral and intellectual feats on a par with men was, apart from anything else, simply unjustified, given that they were judged on an unfair playing field from the outset. Equal access to education would at least determine whether or not women were capable of developing virtuous intellectual and moral character. Of course, such access, Wollstonecraft maintained, was also a woman's right.

Access to education is an epistemic right. It is violated by those who unjustifiably disregard duties to provide access to education, particularly where such disregard disproportionately impacts on a particular group. As Wollstonecraft's efforts indicate, the effects of widespread epistemic rights violations, such as exclusion from education, can have a profound impact on the intellectual character of individuals. This is a secondary epistemic harm that is still as relevant and pressing in many parts of the world today as it was in Britain in the eighteenth century.

This is, of course, a harm to communities, as much as to individuals. When individual members of a community are held back from developing intellectual character, the community as a whole is epistemically disadvantaged. Such communities are failing to make use of the full range of epistemic resources available to them. In eighteenth century Britain, a full 50% of the intellectual muscle of the nation was left underdeveloped and underutilised. The situation is made worse when intellectual vices, such as arrogance and dogmatism, are also cultivated.

Much more can (and I think should) be said about the impact of epistemic rights violations on intellectual character, particularly in relation to exclusionary education practices and the widespread propagation of misinformation in the media. There is not space to explore these themes in detail here. The central claim is that intellectual character is more likely to flourish when individuals, and indeed communities, are exposed to information, knowledge and truth, as opposed to when they are kept ignorant through lack of education or through systematic exposure to misinformation, falsehoods and lies.[63] These barriers to cultivating intellectual character, in the form of epistemic rights violations, constitute an important secondary epistemic harm. This harm compounds the other secondary epistemic harms, including undermining individual's confidence in their beliefs and intellectual abilities, degrading trust in epistemic communities, and reducing the capacity for informed deliberation and debate.

Secondary harm: Practical

Many of the harms caused by epistemic rights violations are not as 'purely' epistemic as those just discussed. There are also numerous practical harms. To reiterate, the distinction between epistemic and practical harms is not clear-cut and is useful primarily as a means of broadly cataloguing types of harm. One of the most pervasive practical harms provides a good illustration of this extensive grey area: diminished decision-making. Diminished decision-making is a practical harm insofar as decision-making is, in essence, a practical capacity. Decision-making is, however, also an epistemic capacity insofar as it relies on access to epistemic goods. What one knows and understands, and the information that is available, will regularly, perhaps typically feature in one's decision-making. As a familiar and important capacity, decision-making reflects the close interconnectedness of the practical and the epistemic domains in everyday life.

Diminished decision-making is a pervasive secondary harm caused by epistemic rights violations. What we believe based on the

---

63 On the relationship between epistemic rights and intellectual character, see also Baehr (2011, p.110).

information we receive affects what we decide to do. When a person's rights to believe, know, understand or be informed about something are violated, she is often left with a limited or corrupted epistemic basis for her decision-making. For example, a woman's beliefs about the risks of abortion will influence whether or not she decides to have one. Indeed, this is something attested to in the official information resource of the Texas Department of Health and Human Services, entitled 'A Woman's Right To Know':

> The decisions you make about your pregnancy are very important – you have the right to make them based upon your values, your beliefs and your health care needs.
>
> (*Texas Department of Health and Human Services*, 2016, p.1)

The resource states that decision-making in relation to abortion is a woman's right and her beliefs are recognised an important part of the decision-making process. This makes perfect sense. Indeed, if this were not the case, the targeted misinformation dispensed in State-mandated informational resources (including this one) would constitute a wasted and relatively harmless effort. But it does not. A woman's ability to make a decision about whether or not to have an abortion is influenced by her beliefs regarding abortion. As such, her decision-making capacity is diminished if she forms false beliefs about the risks of abortion as a result of the violation of her right to information about these risks.

Similarly, a doctor's beliefs about the effectiveness and addictive properties of opioids will influence whether or not she prescribes them to patients. A patient's beliefs about these things, based in part on the trust she places in her doctor, will influence whether and how she decides to take them. Again, if this were not the case, the extensive efforts of pharmaceutical companies like Purdue Pharma to convince doctors of the benefits and low-risk of OxyContin would amount to an excessive and expensive waste of their time. But with the all too real consequences currently playing out in American courts and lives, it is clear that these efforts have been highly effective. They rely on influencing beliefs, above all else. Diminished decision-making is a significant secondary harm of epistemic rights violations.

The secondary practical harm caused by epistemic rights violations can and often does extend beyond diminished decision-making. There are numerous practical consequences of any decision that we make, each of which has the potential to amount to further harm. These consequences can be life-changing. Abortion is an apt example.

If a woman's decision to have or not to have an abortion is based on misinformation, then the source of that misinformation bears at least partial responsibility for any harm that is caused as a result of the decision, given that it was at least partly based on the misinformation they provided. This is true for any harms arising from decisions made as a result of epistemic rights violations. The harms caused by diminished decision-making as a result of these violations reach into every corner of our lives and range from minor to devastating. These include physical, psychological, emotional and sexual harms.

Take, for example, the physical harm caused to individuals by smoking. For a significant number of people, the decision to smoke has or will result in life-changing illness or death. It is now widely known that the tobacco industry was aware of the physical harms of smoking, even in its earliest marketing of tobacco, and that it supressed and withheld this information from the public (Campbell, 2009; Proctor, 2011). As Proctor (2011) puts it "The tobacco makers are notorious masters of deception; they know how to manufacture ignorance and to rewrite history" (p.1). Many of those who took up smoking in the years before information and evidence about serious physical harms became widely available may have made a different decision, had they been given this information. The physical harms suffered by those people are the result of epistemic rights violations perpetrated by the tobacco industry. The same can of course be said today of the serious physical harms caused by opioid addiction and abuse.

The harms in these cases are, moreover, not limited to physical harms. Addiction is also a form of psychological harm. Numerous OxyContin patients have testified to the harmful psychological effects of the opioid, including becoming obsessed with the next dose before the prescribed 12-hour window, anxiety and distress associated with pain and withdrawal, and thoughts of suicide.[64] A former athlete and public school teacher in the US describes his experience of OxyContin in the *LA Times* exposé, quoted previously:

> "The first six hours, it is awesome," he said. Then the effect began to "teeter off" and he became preoccupied with his next dose: "That's all you think about. Your whole day revolves around that"... "Death was looking real good to me."[65]

---

64 https://www.latimes.com/projects/oxycontin-part1/ [Accessed: 11 June 2020].
65 https://www.latimes.com/projects/oxycontin-part1/ [Accessed: 11 June 2020].

These effects represent a distinctively psychological harm. The *LA Times* article also quotes one OxyContin user who felt she must have been 'going nuts' after experiencing pain and withdrawal before the prescribed 12-hour window: "I am really falling apart from the anxiety."[66] This kind of experience illustrates the psychological harm caused by the gas-lighting effects of epistemic rights violations. Alongside epistemic harms, both physical and psychological harms are caused by epistemic rights violations.

This does not amount to claiming that those responsible for the suppression of information about the physical and psychological harms of tobacco, opioids, or any number of other cases, bear the full weight of responsibility for all of the harms caused as a result of smoking, opioid abuse or whatever else. Such a claim would be overblown and is at any rate unnecessary for establishing the gravity and significance of the harms for which these actors are in fact responsible. We know, for example, that people still take up smoking, despite active campaigns aimed at informing people about the risks and common knowledge that it can and does lead to significant physical harm and addiction. In the UK in 2018, 14.7% of people aged over 18 were smokers.[67] This is, nonetheless, a significant decrease from 1974, when the *Office for National Statistics* first began recording figures and found that 45% of the British public were smokers.[68]

We can plausibly infer that when tobacco was first being marketed, a proportion of people would still have taken up smoking even if they had had all of the information regarding the risks. Likewise, in the ever brightening light of information about the harmful effects of opioids such as OxyContin, some doctors will no doubt continue to over-prescribe them and some patients will continue to abuse them. People have many and varied reasons for the choices that they make and misinformation, even when it is extensive, deliberate and pernicious, is not always the cause or culprit of the harms caused as a result of those choices. What the smoking example tells us, however, is that the number of people who would make different choices in light of accurate information about potential risks to their physical

66 https://www.latimes.com/projects/oxycontin-part1/ [Accessed: 11 June 2020].
67 https://www.ons.gov.uk/peoplepopulationandcommunity/healthandsocialcare/healthandlifeexpectancies/bulletins/adultsmokinghabitsingreatbritain/2018 [Accessed: 11 June 2020].
68 https://www.theguardian.com/society/2014/oct/07/smoking-falls-lowest-level-uk-recording-started-1940s [Accessed: 11 June 2020].

and psychological wellbeing is potentially very large. The responsibility is, therefore, correspondingly large for those who perpetrate epistemic rights violations leading to physical and psychological harm.

Emotional harm is another type of secondary harm that can arise from epistemic rights violations. Emotional harm is distinct from psychological harm and characterised by negative effects on a person's emotional wellbeing, including, for example, feelings of guilt or shame resulting from the manipulation of emotions. Consider the emotionally loaded information in the State-mandated women's right to know resources, provided to women considering an abortion. Again, the Texas information resource provides an illustration. The first page of the resource informs a woman:

> the doctor who agrees to perform the abortion must first perform a sonogram, allow you to see your baby, describe the features that can be seen and have you listen to the heartbeat if it can be heard.
>
> (*Texas Department of Health and Human Services*, 2016, p.1)

These are likely to be emotionally loaded experiences for a woman considering an abortion and the language used to describe them has the potential to exacerbate this. This includes describing the foetus as a baby, despite a later concession that "Your baby is scientifically referred to as an embryo" (p.3). The resource also states that "Newborn babies are able to feel pain. We know that babies develop the ability to feel pain while in the womb" (p.3) and, under the section entitled 'Making an Informed Decision', it explains "Your doctor will describe the baby growing in your womb to you and give you a list of agencies that offer alternatives to abortion" (p.10). A plausible reading of this language is that it is designed to manipulate a woman's feelings about the act and consequences of abortion, in order to influence her decision.

Emotionally loaded language is common on both sides of the abortion debate. Either you "know that every baby deserves protection and that abortion breaks God's heart"[69] or you believe in "the fundamental human right of all people to make their own decisions about their lives."[70] In either case, the implication is both that there

---

69 https://www.care-net.org/ [Accessed: 06 Sep 2019].
70 https://www.prochoiceamerica.org/issue/abortion-access/ [Accessed: 06 Sep 2019].

is a straightforward answer to the question of abortion and that the issue matters deeply. Given the latter, it makes sense to be emotionally invested in one's views on abortion. This emotional investment, however, leaves many open to emotional harm, particularly those faced with a decision about abortion, who may experience this as an emotionally vulnerable time. Moreover, the debate itself is typically characterised as deeply polarised and reflective of fundamental human values. Arguably, this representation of the debate contributes to emotional manipulation on both 'sides'.

To be clear, the use and abuse of emotional language is not restricted to cases of lies and misinformation. A person's emotions can be manipulated as easily by the truth as by falsehoods. Regardless, emotionally loaded language has the potential to result in, for example, feelings of guilt and shame for a woman considering abortion. When emotional harm, such as this, is the result of the use of emotional language in a context of misinformation, then the misinformation is at least partly the cause of the emotional harm. In other words, a woman who is made to feel guilty about considering an abortion because of misleading information is suffering from emotional harm that is the result of an epistemic rights violation. Epistemic rights violations can cause emotional harm.

A final, secondary practical harm that can result from epistemic rights violations is sexual harm. This may arise, for example, when a person is deceived into having sex. Dougherty (2013) maintains that a person is deceived into sex when they have sex on the basis of a lie or false information which serves as a 'deal-breaker' for their decision to have sex. In other words, had they known the truth, they would have chosen not to have sex. He argues that a serious wrong has taken place when this happens because "someone has the right down to the very last detail what comes into sexual contact with her body, and this is a particularly important right" (p.744). Deceiving someone into having sex is a violation of her right to bodily autonomy. Dougherty emphasises that "the serious wrong here is the non-consensual sex, rather than the deception itself" (p.740). However, it is the deception that makes the sex non-consensual meaning that epistemic rights violations are a direct cause of harm in these cases. As observed, this harm may be life-changing if the deception concerns a sexually transmitted disease, such as HIV.

Returning, then, to the case of AIDS denialism in South Africa, in addition to the physical harms caused by epistemic rights violations, there is evidence that AIDS denialism has led to risky sexual behaviours. Grebe and Nattrass (2011) used a large-scale, longitudinal study to examine the relationship between behaviours and attitudes towards AIDS and AIDS denialist beliefs in South Africa in the 2000s:

> the odds of using a condom were halved amongst female African AIDS conspiracy believers, whereas for African men, never having heard of TAC [Treatment Action Campaign, the pro-science activist group that opposed Mbeki on AIDS] and holding AIDS denialist beliefs were the key determinants of unsafe sex.
>
> (Grebe and Nattrass, 2011, p.1)

For South Africans during the key years of AIDS denialism, belief in AIDS denialism was strongly related to increased probability of engaging in unsafe sex. As Chigwedere and Essex (2010) put it:

> AIDS denialists are dangerous to the general population; many have been persuaded into risky behaviors, ineffective alternative remedies, and other harmful actions.
>
> (Chigwedere and Essex, 2010, p.243)

Risky sexual behaviours can and often do amount to sexual harm. As such, when epistemic rights violations lead to risky sexual behaviours, they too can cause sexual harm.

Epistemic rights violations can lead to a range of secondary practical harms, including physical, psychological, emotional and sexual harm. In addition, epistemic rights violations lead to primary and secondary epistemic harms. These harms range from minor to devastating. From epistemic anguish, to the impacts of life-changing decisions, to illness and death. As illustrated through the many and varied cases discussed, these harms extend into every arena of public and private life. In short, everyone is at risk from epistemic rights violations, everyone can get hurt. This concludes investigation of the focal question of this chapter. There can, I think, be little question of the serious and significant harms caused by epistemic rights violations.

Summary

In this chapter, I have characterised and catalogued the harms caused by epistemic rights violations. In addition, I have examined the relationship between epistemic rights violations and epistemic injustice. Many of the harms caused by epistemic rights violations are also common to contexts of epistemic injustice. These harms include two forms of primary epistemic harm: 'epistemic injury' and 'epistemic insult'.

Epistemic injuries put an individual or community at an epistemic disadvantage, while epistemic insults wrong them in their capacity as an epistemic agent.

Secondary harms include 'more purely' epistemic harms and practical harms. The former include undermining a person's beliefs or intellectual abilities and inhibiting the development of her intellectual character. These also impact epistemic communities, putting the community as a whole at an epistemic disadvantage through lack of intellectual virtue and the presence of intellectual vice, as well as leading to degradation of trust among community members and reducing capacity for informed deliberation and debate. The secondary practical harms include physical, psychological, emotional and sexual harms.

To reiterate the simple take home message of the chapter and, to some extent, the book: epistemic rights violations cause harm. These harms are many and varied. They can be widespread, profound and fatal. Such harms are as old as lies and deceit themselves. However, in the fast-paced, crowded and information-centric world of the twenty-first century, they are perhaps more pernicious and more damaging than ever before. This leads naturally to the final question: why do we need epistemic rights?

5 Why do we need epistemic rights?

The preceding chapters have offered a short but rigorous exposition of epistemic rights. The title question of this chapter asks, in essence, why this exposition has been necessary. Why do we need this concept and the vocabulary that comes with it? In many respects, this is the first question of the book, rather than the last; the question that serves as motivation for writing it. In order to answer it, however, an analysis of the concept has been required. What are epistemic rights and what do they do? These questions were addressed in Chapters 1 and 2. Epistemic rights mandate actions and omissions in order to protect epistemic right-holders from the harms caused by epistemic rights violations. The nature and extent of these violations and harms were discussed in Chapters 3 and 4. Understanding these is also integral to appreciating the value and necessity of epistemic rights. The book as a whole, then, serves as an answer to the question in the title of this chapter. It is nonetheless worth articulating, in these final pages, a concise answer to this question, drawing on the work that has already been done and highlighting several key points.

A unified class of rights

Epistemic rights are rights. In Chapter 1, I argued that epistemic rights are as substantive as any other rights, spanning the full Hohfeldian schema and existing within a broader framework of legal and moral rights. I have sought to position epistemic rights as a unified class of rights within that framework. This is important. Many of the examples involve epistemic rights that are already recognised as rights in some other sense. The right that I have to know my blood sugar levels after being tested for diabetes is a right that I have in my capacity as a patient, as well as in my capacity as an epistemic agent. The same can be said of the rights that OxyContin patients have to accurate information about the drug. If patients are (at least in principle) protected in virtue of patient rights, why do we need epistemic rights?

Why highlight the epistemic dimension and treat it as constituting a fully-fledged right, in and of itself? In other words, why identify epistemic rights as a distinct and unified class of rights? There are, I think, three good reasons. Firstly, treating epistemic rights as a distinct and unified class effectively names and identifies a feature of our moral landscape, allowing us to more accurately describe and better understand it. Secondly, it allows for the identification of previously unrecognised or underappreciated harms and puts us in a better position to detect new ones. Thirdly, it allows for the design of more effective protections against those harms, in the form of education, regulation and legislation. These three reasons are interrelated; an illustration will help.

Take the primary example used by Fricker (2007, Chapter 7) to illustrate hermeneutical injustice: sexual harassment. Sexual harassment can take many and varied forms, from subtle looks and gestures, to comments, jokes and innuendo, to acts of physical threat and violence. Recognising that these harms are unified under the concept of sexual harassment has had important consequences. Firstly, it names and identifies a feature of our moral landscape, allowing women, in particular, to more accurately describe and better understand their situation, including previously unacknowledged and unspoken feelings and experiences. Recognising these common experiences as falling under the concept of sexual harassment diminishes feelings of isolation and alienation, and undermines ideas of being 'crazy' or delusional.

Secondly, the concept of sexual harassment has allowed for the identification of previously unrecognised and underappreciated harms, as well as the detection of new ones. Many of the subtler forms of sexual harassment, such as inappropriate gestures and jokes, are now recognised as harms in a way that would not have been possible without the ability to identify them as instances of the more general concept. New harms are also identified in this way, for example, the practice of 'upskirting', which involves taking a picture under another person's clothing without their permission.

Thirdly, the recognition of these harms has led to the existence of significantly greater (although still imperfect) protections against sexual harassment. These have come in the form of better understanding and education surrounding the experiences and effects of sexual harassment, as well as regulation and legislation. Upskirting was recently made a criminal offence in the UK.[71]

The unification of diverse behaviours and actions under the concept of sexual harassment has led to improved understanding,

---

71 https://www.gov.uk/government/news/upskirting-law-comes-into-force [Accessed: 08 Dec 2020].

identification and protection in relation to a particular set of harms. Likewise, by treating epistemic rights as a distinct and unified class of rights, we stand to gain from improved understanding, identification and protection in relation to harms arising in the epistemic domain. As I have emphasised, epistemic rights are present across diverse arenas of public and private life. It is not, therefore, surprising to find the term 'right to know' distributed across these. It is, however, notable that the term is always deployed in the particular, rather than as an instance of a more general class of rights. Even when different sets of laws in the same country are referred to as 'right to know laws', as is the case in the US with worker's and women's rights to know, there is little, beyond the phrase itself, to identify these as instances of a more general and unified legal or moral class. By treating epistemic rights as a distinct and unified class, one can place such instances in a broader framework, improving our understanding of the complex picture that they are part of and facilitating connections between areas of contemporary life that may seem otherwise disparate.

This unification in the epistemic domain is, I believe, critical for understanding and describing the moral landscape of the twenty-first century. Trying to understand it without this epistemic dimension is like trying to understand a physical landscape with a map missing important topographical features. You might plan a 10-mile hike, unaware that you will be walking steeply uphill, and so fail to bring enough water or budget enough time before sunset. Before you know it, you are dehydrated, disoriented and walking in the dark. In much the same way, one might identify a moral harm but fail to recognise or have the resources to understand and articulate an important epistemic dimension. One is left disoriented and unable to fully comprehend, describe or process the harm itself. Epistemic rights (and epistemic duties) provide a simple and powerful way to do this.

In addition, treating epistemic rights as a distinct and unified class allows for the identification of previously unrecognised or underappreciated harms and puts us in a better position to detect new ones. As soon as one identifies individual instances of the right to know as falling under a unified class of rights, one starts to notice gaps – places where epistemic rights have not yet been identified and should be. Why, for example, do worker's right to know laws in the US pertain to information about harmful chemicals, but not about any number of other risks? When viewed in terms of the unified class, these right to know laws seem like an oddly restrictive application of a much more widely available concept. The same can be said of the other disparate right to know laws that I have described.

Furthermore, technological advances in our abilities to collect, communicate, disseminate, withhold and distort information have made previously unimagined harms possible and, in some cases, commonplace (as well as providing for previously unimagined solutions and opportunities). The kind of global surveillance exposed by Snowden would have been impossible mere decades ago. This has given rise to new questions and challenges, many of which concern the allocation and abuse of epistemic rights and duties. The questions addressed in Chapter 3, for example, concerning the moral and legal protection of epistemic rights, are central to determining the type and level of protection needed in any given case.

The ability to articulate these questions and challenges in terms of epistemic rights allows for the design of more effective protections against the harms caused by epistemic rights violations in the form of education, regulation and legislation. While progress has undoubtedly been made on these fronts, the contemporary world is evolving fast and many of the new and pervasive harms that we see involve the use and abuse of information, knowledge, truth etc. The distinct and unified class of epistemic rights constitutes a ready-made resource that can be put to work in the face of these harms to provide epistemic protections that are fit for purpose in the twenty-first century.

That is not to say that the need for such protections is new or unique to twenty-first century life. The notion of fake news, for example, which has gathered renewed currency in recent years, has given rise to new efforts to protect readers, listeners and viewers from a range of harms. However, similar efforts were central to the campaign for press freedom in the US, following the Second World War. Speaking in 1945, former *Associated Press* Executive Director, Kent Cooper said:

> The contribution toward war that false news has generated is as amazing in its extent as it is little understood... There were other evil elements that contributed to the war spirit. The control and perversion of news in Germany was certainly one. Indeed, I know of no other one for which a warning was given at an opportune time but which was not heeded at all. It could have been heeded.[72]

In his work, Cooper highlighted some of the most damaging, widespread and intractable epistemic rights violations of his moment. His concerns

---

72 https://timesmachine.nytimes.com/timesmachine/1945/01/22/88184102.pdf [Accessed: 3 December 2019].

are disconcertingly salient 75 years on. Cooper also placed epistemic rights at the heart of the solution, asserting, in the same speech: "if we are to develop a peaceful world the people must have the right to know the truth about each other".[73] This is as true now as it was in 1945. Yet the notion of the people's right to know remains problematically underspecified. Writing in 1953, W.M. Beaney commented, "the people's "right to know" is unquestionably one of the most narrowly defined and least effectively protected rights" (1953, p.1176). Over fifty years later, Richardson (2004), makes a similar point:

> In fighting the battle for access, we have failed to distinguish adequately – in our own minds and in the minds of audiences, public officials, and jurists – the difference between the legal right to access and a moral right to know.
>
> (Richardson, 2004, p.46)

Richardson rightly highlights the underappreciated distinction between legal and moral bases for epistemic rights in the domain of press freedom. A journalist's legal right (or not) to access information is not synonymous with her moral right (or not) to access that information or to publish it. The complex question of how these rights should be allocated and, therefore, how they should be protected, is obscured by invocation of an oversimplified construal of the people's right to know. Both of these rights are, nonetheless, members of the distinct and unified class of epistemic rights. Examining their place within the wider class, including their relationship to each other, to other epistemic rights and to other legal and moral rights, will lead to a more sophisticated appreciation of the 'people's right to know', and to better protection of it in legal and moral terms.

Of course, the people's right to know is just one, albeit prominent example of an epistemic right worthy of more nuanced treatment. Cooper focused exclusively on the people's right to know as it pertained to the mass media and freedom of the press. A review of his 1956 book on the topic picks up on this restricted focus. The reviewer, Bixler (1957), writes:

> The concept of "the right to know" would surely cover not only the daily press, radio, television and the movies, which Cooper

---

73 https://timesmachine.nytimes.com/timesmachine/1945/01/22/88184102.pdf [Accessed: 3 December 2019].

explicitly includes, but the publishing of books and magazines, which, perhaps inadvertently, he does not. It would appear also to offer protection to the work of libraries, schools, research institutes, adult education, foundations "for the public welfare" – in fact, to any operation devoted to the discovery of new truth or to the dissemination of knowledge and opinion.

(Bixler, 1957, p.115)

Here one finds an appeal for a wider application of the right to know than even Cooper had envisioned. One that pertains not only to a particular domain, such as the media, or to a particular subset of the population, such as workers, women, children etc., but rather to the epistemic dimension itself, in its manifestation throughout our lives. In other words, an appeal for a distinct and unified class of epistemic rights. This book serves as an overdue response to that appeal. Treating epistemic rights as a distinct and unified class can lead to improved understanding, identification and protection across every arena of our lives, in relation to a range of immediate and often significant harms.

The language of rights

The argument that epistemic rights constitute a distinct and unified class speaks to the significance of the epistemic in our lives. There is, however, another question that is, in some sense, more fundamental: why appeal to the language of rights, at all? Why draw on the notion of rights and duties to expose and articulate the epistemic wrongs described in Chapter 3 and the epistemic harms described in Chapter 4? What is the language of rights adding to this picture?

There is a simple answer to this question and it is one that I have reiterated throughout the book: epistemic rights are rights. As such, the language of rights is the only language that can do the job of accurately describing the phenomenon in question. That language is not, however, without its critics (Milner, 1989; Glendon, 1991; Pieterse, 2007) and the question, therefore, deserves deeper consideration than this simple answer provides.

There are three good reasons for employing the language of rights in the epistemic domain. Firstly, rights allow for the direction of conduct in a unique and consistent way – they prescribe what we and others can and cannot do. Secondly, rights constitute a basis and a mechanism for holding those responsible for harms and wrongs to account on both legal and moral grounds. Thirdly, the language of rights has a distinctive rhetorical force that, when used appropriately, is invaluable for the advancement and protection of ourselves and our communities. As before, these three reasons are interrelated.

Firstly, rights provide constraints on behaviour, determining what we can and cannot permissibly do according to either morality or the law (or both). This is an important and distinctive feature of rights. Hart (1955) makes this point when he considers moral systems that do not include the notion of rights. He comments that in such systems:

> [no] argument [could] be constructed to show that, from the bare fact that actions were recognized as ones which ought or ought not to be done, as right, wrong, good or bad, it followed that some specific kind of conduct fell under these categories.
>
> (Hart, 1955, p.177)

The language of rights allows for the direction of conduct in a unique way. This draws on the point about rights that was made in Chapter 1: rights pertain to actions and omissions. Thus, asserting one's rights is not merely a way of identifying right and wrong, good and bad, it amounts to directing the conduct of others and demanding that they act in certain ways.

This unique feature of the language is particularly significant in the case of epistemic rights, given that the epistemic domain is often under-regulated and under-legislated. Evidence of this is found in the numerous examples of epistemic rights violations that I have discussed (and many others that I have not). In the majority of these cases, harmful epistemic conduct has gone unchecked and unchallenged. Epistemic duties are not well distributed (or even recognised) and those who bear them are not easily held to account. The language of epistemic rights has distinctive force in light of this, allowing for the direction of epistemic conduct in a unique and consistent way across disparate contexts and concerns.

This leads to the second reason for employing the language of rights. Rights constitute a basis and a mechanism for holding those responsible for harms and wrongs to account on both legal and moral grounds. One must, however, use the language in order to see this in action. I said in Chapter 3, that even in cases where epistemic rights have direct or indirect legal protection, it is not the case that the term 'epistemic rights' is used in the law. The language of rights, however, is a common feature of legal discourse and appeals to rights in legal practice are commonplace, ranging from consumer rights to human rights and many in between. The absence of the term epistemic rights in this picture represents a notable gap in the legal terrain. Legal discourse and practice can be enriched by talk of epistemic rights. In turn, the legal frameworks and procedures that are already in place to protect many other forms of right can be brought to bear in the epistemic domain, once the language of epistemic rights is in use. This is especially important in light of the more intangible manifestations of widespread harms and injustice resulting from epistemic rights violations. The role of such violations in the US opioid crisis, mass human rights atrocities, and AIDS denialism in South Africa provide only a few stark illustrations of just how widespread and damaging these harms can be and yet still go insufficiently accounted for, in many (perhaps the most) important respects. A lengthy extract from a paper, 'AIDS denialism and public health practice' (Chigwedere and Essex, 2010), is worth quoting in full, to underline this point:

> Mbeki implemented negligent policies that led to the premature death of hundreds of thousands. His reasons, as stated by himself and health minister Tshabalala-Msimang, were that he questioned whether HIV causes AIDS and whether ARVs [antiretrovirals] are safe, and neither ever publicly backed down from this thinking. The science behind Mbeki was Duesberg and other denialists. Duesberg is still arguing for AIDS denialism and defending Mbeki and the policies that led to more than 330,000 deaths. By any reasonable standard, this requires some form of accountability. Seth Kalichman has likened the AIDS denialists to the Holocaust deniers [Kalichman, 2009] and Edwin Cameron likened letting AIDS patients die without medications to those who silently enabled the evils of Nazi Germany and apartheid South Africa to go unchecked [Cameron, 2005]. John Moore and Nathan Geffen have called for AIDS denialists to be put on trial [Moore 2009; Geffen 2009] and Mark Wainberg has argued that denialists should be charged with public endangerment and "people like Peter Duesberg belong in jail" [Wainberg, 2004]. Zachie Achmat has called for a commission of enquiry such as the Truth and Reconciliation Commission that was tasked with handling the apartheid era crimes.[74] For how are South Africans ever going to trust their health system again? How can a modern government be penetrated by denialists to the extent of

implementing policies that kill hundreds of thousands? William Makgoba suggested that impeding AIDS treatment was collaborating in committing genocide,[75] and Wycliffe Muga has asked whether Mbeki's killing of 330,000 by obstructing life-saving medications is much different from Sudan's President al Bashir's killing a similar number in Darfur through obstructing humanitarian aid and militias [Muga, 2009]. Is this not a crime against humanity? Does the International Criminal Court not have a role, for it was established to handle those cases where national courts may be unable or unwilling to prosecute?[76] Whatever the most appropriate avenue is, what seems apparent is the need for accountability.

(Chigwedere and Essex, 2010, p.243)

It is, I think, both striking and important to emphasise that the extensive and profound harms detailed in this powerful extract originate in the violation of epistemic rights. No doubt there are other factors in play, but at its core this case, and many others like it, centres on brazen and unjustifiable disregard for epistemic duties. The language of epistemic rights and duties allows us to understand and articulate this fact and provides a basis and a mechanism for holding those responsible for the relevant, often widespread and intangible harms and wrongs to account on both legal and moral grounds.

This connects with the third reason for employing the language of rights. Such accountability is made possible, in part, because of the distinctive rhetorical force that accompanies rights-talk. When used appropriately, this is invaluable for the advancement and protection of ourselves and our communities, in many arenas of life. Moreover, the language of rights is by now a familiar language to most, especially in the Western liberal democracies where it has been primarily championed. This familiarity enables easy uptake of rights language by diverse groups for the purposes of progress and its efficacy is reinforced by appeal to rights in legal discourse and practice.

As such, for many, it will not take much to understand the concept of a 'right to know' or to use it. It would not, for example, sound odd or unnatural for me to argue that I have a right to know my blood sugar

---

75 Quoted in The Guardian, 2001 Jun 12. Available at: http://www. guardian.co.uk/world/2001/jun/12/aids.chrismcgreal.

76 International Criminal Court. Available at: http://www.icc-cpi. int/about/Official_Journal.html.

levels after being tested for diabetes, especially if I find out that my doctor has been lying to me about them. Similarly, it would not sound odd for me to argue that my doctor had no right to reveal my test results to a stranger in the street. Talk of epistemic rights, whilst not talked of as epistemic rights, is commonplace in ordinary language. David Coady (2010) makes this point compellingly in a discussion of the right to know:

> It seems clear that our ordinary thought about rights includes this concept, as when we say, for example, that a patient has a right to know his or her medical condition, that a soldier has a right to know the cause for which he [or she] is fighting, or that the public has the right to know about some of the activities of certain public figures.
>
> (Coady, 2010, pp.105–6).

These rights, and many others that find easy expression in ordinary language, are bound together by their concern with epistemic goods. This is both a natural way to group such rights and a powerful way to articulate them. The availability of this familiar language, with a distinctive rhetorical force, is invaluable for capturing the nature and significance of epistemic rights. This is perhaps especially so given the natural obscurity of some of the more technical language that is characteristic of academic epistemology.

Indeed, the power and political force of rights language is, I think, one of the most compelling reasons to adopt it in the epistemic domain. This language has been employed, to noteworthy effect, in confronting many deep and widespread injustices over the past one hundred years alone. It is no mistake that Wollstonecraft (1792) expressed her appeal for equality between the sexes in terms of rights. In most cases, these injustices are still being fought in one way or another, and the language of rights continues to be deployed: women's rights, black rights, disability rights, LGBTQ rights, trans rights etc. The language of rights has proven to be a powerful tool in the face of widespread harms and injustice. There is no reason for it not to be deployed in the epistemic domain.

Of course, not all groups that deploy the language of rights do so in good faith. Rights-talk is open to abuse precisely because it is both powerful and familiar. A prominent critic of rights-talk in the US, Glendon (1991), writes that "the prominence of a certain kind of rights talk in our political discussions is both a symptom of, and a contributing factor to ... disorder in the body politic" (p.2). Nonetheless, she argues, "what is needed is not the abandonment, but the renewal, of our strong rights tradition" (p.4). The fact that the language of rights is open to abuse is not a reason to cease using it, but rather a reason to ensure that its use is rooted in the common good. I have tried to demonstrate that epistemic rights-talk is, indeed, rooted in the common good.

When used appropriately, the language of epistemic rights has a distinctive rhetorical force that is invaluable for the advancement and protection of ourselves and our communities. Moreover, as noted, this language allows for the direction of epistemic conduct in a unique and consistent way, across diverse arenas of life, and constitutes a basis and a mechanism for holding those responsible for harms and wrongs to account, on legal and moral grounds.

Knowing matters

There are few, I think, who would argue that the epistemic dimension of our lives doesn't matter. This is perhaps especially so in recent years when the threats of widespread misinformation, distortion and obfuscation of the truth, deception and outright lies have become a particularly potent topic of public concern. It is no coincidence that epistemology has changed significantly in the past two decades, and perhaps most dramatically in only the past five years. Epistemologists are increasingly concerned with the social and political dimensions of the epistemic, in a mirroring of the public's increased concern with the epistemic dimensions of the social and political.

The concept of epistemic rights is particularly apt in this contemporary setting. Epistemic rights arise within and are bound by epistemic communities comprised of individuals with different epistemic abilities, opportunities and duties. As such, one's epistemic rights are inextricably tied to the social and political world that one inhabits as an epistemic agent. Moreover, epistemic rights serve to highlight the active nature of the epistemic within our social, political and, ultimately, moral landscape. The violation of rights is something that people *do* to each other. Recognising that sometimes the rights that are violated are *epistemic* rights, allows us to understand the active and sometimes harmful force of the epistemic in our lives and communities. Knowledge and ignorance can empower and disempower, lies can subjugate, misinformation can harm. The concept of epistemic rights reflects the close alignment between the epistemic, moral and political dimensions of our lives, allowing us to more accurately describe and better understand their interrelatedness within the complex social world in which we live.

As such, the concept and its analysis provides an opportunity to articulate new and pressing questions and to examine old questions in new ways. I have addressed some of these questions throughout the book. If I have done what I set out to do, many more questions will have been prompted by the preceding pages. There is certainly more to be said about the nature, scope and value of epistemic rights. As Thomas Nagel (1995) writes:

> Contrary to the suggestion of the *Declaration of Independence*, rights are not self-evident: They require precise argument, definition, and adjustment, which will always give rise to controversy, and there is room for very considerable disagreement and development in the details of their design.
>
> (Nagel, 1995, p.84)

No doubt, then, that there is room for considerable disagreement and development concerning the nature, content and scope of epistemic rights.

Nonetheless, the suite of contemporary cases that I have drawn on throughout the book, and the literally hundreds of others that I have encountered while writing it, illustrate that widespread harms and injustice are as real and damaging in the epistemic domain as in any other. These cases demonstrate a pressing need for greater protection and accountability. One need only consider the deliberate and systematic misinformation campaigns of major corporations, political parties and mass media outlets. *There is no question* that extensive epistemic rights violations take place. *There is no question* that we are all subject to them. *There is no question* that they harm. The examples I have drawn on represent a tiny fragment of the reality of this in the twenty-first century.

Epistemic rights, of course, cannot be expected to do all of the work. They are just one, albeit significant, feature of the moral landscape. Perhaps there is call for an epistemic Hippocratic Oath – a pledge to *do no epistemic harm* – taken by those who bear epistemic duties in their professional roles and who, thereby, serve as key actors in the epistemic ecosystem of the twenty-first century. Our teachers, lawyers, doctors, scientists, authors, academics, librarians, social media moguls, salespeople, advertising executives, politicians, leaders and journalists. Whilst not itself a form of legal accountability, an epistemic Hippocratic Oath seems to capture something that is both central and essential to the protection of ourselves and our communities.[77]

Such a pledge, of course, represents only one of many possible defences. Some of these are already in place in specific arenas and could be effectively extended, others are yet to be imagined in light of both present and future harms and wrongs. There is certainly a place for greater epistemic activism (Medina, 2021) and a more rigorous and wide-ranging public debate concerning the harms and wrongs that occur in the epistemic domain. Whatever else, it is clear that the battle to defend epistemic rights can and should be fought on multiple fronts. The attacks, after all, are coming from all sides.

Indeed, the world is now grappling with the many and varied challenges posed by the Covid-19 pandemic. Covid-19 has changed many aspects of our lives and communities in both striking and subtle ways. Ultimately, the crisis is one of life and death but the role that information and misinformation play are significant for precisely this reason. If we cannot access the truth, or trust the individuals and institutions whose responsibility it is to seek out and distribute it, then we are vulnerable to the wide range of harms that I have described in this book, in addition to the dangers that the pandemic itself presents. The concept of epistemic rights offers a valuable resource to meet the epistemic challenges that we face in times of crisis, such as this, and beyond.

As I write, I sit a short distance from *The Sackler Centre for Developmental Psychobiology*, a division of the Psychiatry Department at the *University of Edinburgh*. It was bestowed upon the university by the owners of Purdue Pharma. There is a certain conflicted irony seeing the name Sackler lauded by the same institution that has principally supported me in the writing of this book. The *University of Edinburgh* states as its vision: "Our graduates, and the knowledge we discover with our partners, make the world a better place."[78] The implicit tension notwithstanding, the university's vision is exactly right: knowledge really can and does make the world a better place in myriad and unexpected ways. Simply put, knowing matters, and that is why we need epistemic rights.

---

77 This idea is inspired by a TED talk, given by journalist Lara Setrakian, the co-founder and CEO of News Deeply, about issues of trust and sensationalism in the media. In it, Setrakian spoke of a Hippocratic Oath for journalists: a binding principle, to which all journalists must commit, to 'do no harm'. Here I extend that principle across the epistemic spectrum of public and private life. The talk is available at https://www.ted.com/talks/lara_setrakian_3_ways_to_fix_a_broken_news_industry [Accessed: 12 June 2020].

78 https://www.ed.ac.uk/about/strategy-2030/our-vision-purpose-and-values [Accessed: 12 June 2020].

Bibliography

Adler, Jonathan. 2002. *Belief's Own Ethics*. Cambridge, MA: MIT Press.

Aguilera, Edgar, R. 2013. Truth and victims' rights: Towards a legal epistemology of international criminal justice. *Mexican Law Review* 6(1): 119–160.

Alston, William, P. 1988. The deontological conception of epistemic justification. *Philosophical Perspectives* 2: 257–299.

Alston, William P. 1989. *Epistemic justification: essays in the theory of knowledge*. Ithaca, NY: Cornell.

Astell, Mary. 2002. *A Serious Proposal to the Ladies. Parts I and II [1694]*, P. Springborg (ed.): 81 and 62. Ontario: Broadview Literary Texts.

Audi, Robert. 1991. Faith, belief, and rationality. *Philosophical Perspectives* 5: 213–239.

Baehr, Jason. 2011. *The Inquiring Mind*. Oxford: Oxford University Press.

Barker-Benfield, G. J. 1992. *The Culture of Sensibility: Sex and Society in Eighteenth Century Britain*. Chicago: University of Chicago Press.

Battaly, Heather. 2015. *Virtue*. Cambridge: Polity Press.

Beaney, W. M. 1953. Review of The People's Right to Know: Legal Access to Public Records and Proceedings. *American Political Science Review* 47(4): 1176.

Besson, Samantha. 2007. Enforcing the child's right to know: Contrasting approaches under the Convention of the Rights of the Child and the European Convention on Human Rights. *International Journal of Law, Policy and the Family* 21: 137–159.

Bixler, Paul. 1957. The Right to Know: An Exposition of the Evils of News Suppression and Propaganda by Kent Cooper. *The Library Quarterly* 27(2): 115.

Blanchard, Margaret, A. 1986. *Exporting the First Amendment: The Press Government Crusade of 1945-1952*. New York: Logman, Inc. White Plains.

Boer, H and Emons, P. 2004. Accurate and inaccurate HIV transmission beliefs, stigmatizing and HIV protection motivation in northern Thailand. *AIDS Care* 16(2): 167–176.

Brown, Étienne. 2018. Propaganda, Misinformation, and the Epistemic Value of Democracy. *Critical Review* 30(3-4): 194–218.

Bryant, A. G., Narasimhan, S., Bryant-Comstock, K. and Levi, E. E. 2014. Crisis pregnancy centre websites: Information, misinformation and disinformation. *Contraception* 90: 601–605.

Căbulea May, Simon. 2015. Directed Duties. *Philosophy Compass* 10(8): 523–532.

Cameron, E. 2005. *Witness to AIDS*. London: I. B. Tauris.

Campbell, Macgregor. 2009. Health Clues Found in Big Tobacco Files. *New Scientist* 202(2713): 8.

Carel, Havi and Kidd, Ian James. 2014. Epistemic injustice in healthcare: a philosophical analysis. *Medicine, Health Care and Philosophy* 17: 529–540.

Chigwedere, Pride, Seage, George, Gruskin, Sofia, Lee, Tun-Hou and Essex, M. 2008. Estimating the Lost Benefits of Antiretroviral Drug Use in South Africa. *Journal of Acquired Immunodeficiency Syndrome* 49(4): 410–415.

Chigwedere, Pride and Essex, M. 2010. AIDS Denialism and Public Health Practice. *AIDS and Behaviour* 14: 237–247.

Chisholm, Roderick, M. 1977. *The Theory of Knowledge*. Englewood Cliffs: Prentice-Hall.

Chisholm, Roderick, M. 1991. Firth and the Ethics of Belief. *Philosophy of Phenomenological Research* 51(1): 119–128.

Cifrino, David, A. 1988. Exporting the First Amendment: The Press Government Crusade of 1945–1952 by Margaret A. Blanchard. *Boston College Third World Law Journal* 9(1): 143–149.

Clifford, William. 1879. The Ethics of Belief. *Clifford's Lectures and Essays*. London: Macmillan, 183.

Coady, David. 2010. Two Concepts of Epistemic Injustice. *Episteme* 7(2): 101–113.

Cohen, Carl. 1997. Do Animals Have Rights? *Ethics & Behavior* 7(2): 91–102.

Conee, Earl. 1987. Evident, but rationally unacceptable. *Australasian Journal of Philosophy* 65: 316–326.

Cooper, Kent. 1956. *The Right to Know: An Exposition of the Evils of News Suppression and Propaganda*. New York: Farrar, Straus & Cudahy.

Cross, Harold. 1953. *The People's Right to Know: Legal Access to Public Records and Proceedings*. New York: Columbia University Press.

Cruft, Rowan. 2004. Rights: Beyond Interest Theory and Will Theory? *Law and Philosophy* 23(4): 347–397.

Cruft, Rowan. 2010. On the Non-Instrumental Value of Basic Rights. *Journal of Moral Philosophy* 7: 441–461.

Cruft, Rowan. 2013. Why is it disrespectful to violate rights? *Proceedings of the Aristotelian Society* 113(2): 201–224.

Cruft Rowan, Liao S M and Renzo M. 2015. The Philosophical Foundations of Human Rights: An Overview. In: Cruft R, Liao S M, Renzo M (eds.). *Philosophical Foundations of Human Rights. Philosophical Foundations of Law*, Oxford: Oxford University Press, 1–41.

Cuillier, David. 2016. The People's Right to Know: Comparing Harold L. Cross' Pre-FOIA World to Post-FOIA Today. *Journal of Communication Law and Policy* 21(4): 433–463.

David, Edward. 2020. *A Christian Approach to Corporate Religious Liberty*. Oxford: Palgrave Macmillan.

Derickson, Alan. 2016. Inventing the Right to Know: Herbert Abrams's Efforts to Democratize Access to Workplace Health Hazard Information in the 1950s. *American Journal of Public Health* 106(2): 237–245.

Donnelly, Jack and Whelan, Daniel, J. (eds.) 2020. *International Human Rights.* New York: Routledge.

Dotson, Kristie. 2011. Tracking Epistemic Violence, Tracking Practices of Silencing. *Hypatia* 26(2): 236–257.

Dotson, Kristie. 2014. Conceptualizing Epistemic Oppression. *Social Epistemology* 28(2): 115–138.

Dougherty, Tom. 2013. Sex, Lies and Consent. *Ethics* 123: 717–744.

Dretske, Fred. 2000. Entitlement: Epistemic rights without epistemic duties? *Philosophy and Phenomenological Research* 60(3): 591–606.

Duesberg, Peter, Koehnlein, Claus and Rasnick, David. 2003. The chemical bases of the various AIDS epidemics: Recreational drugs, anti-viral chemotherapy and malnutrition. *Journal of Biosciences* 28: 383–412.

Essex Max and Mboup Souleymane. 2002. Introduction: The etiology of AIDS. In: Essex M., Mboup S., Kanki P., Marlink R. and Tlou S. (eds.), *AIDS in Africa.* Boston, MA: Springer, 1–10.

European Court of Human Rights. 2019. *Guide on Article 8 of the European Convention on Human Rights.* https://www.echr.coe.int/Documents/Guide_Art_8_ENG.pdf

Feinberg, Joel. 1980. *Rights, Justice, and the Bounds of Liberty.* Princeton: Princeton University Press.

Feinberg, Joel. 2013. The rights of animals and unborn generations. In: Shafer-Landau, Russ (ed.) *Ethical Theory: An Anthology,* 372–380.

Feldman, Richard. 1988. Epistemic obligations. *Philosophical Perspectives* 2: 235–256.

Feldman, Richard. 2005. Epistemological Duties. In: Moser, Paul, K. (ed.) *The Oxford Handbook of Epistemology.* Oxford: Oxford University Press, 362–384.

Ferrer Mac-Gregor, Eduardo. 2016. The right to the truth as an autonomous right under the Inter-American human right system. *Mexican Law Review* 9(1): 121–139.

Fourie, Pieter and Meyer, Melissa. 2011. *The Politics of AIDS Denialism: South Africa's Failure to Respond.* London: Routledge.

Freeman, Michael. 2017. *Human Rights.* Cambridge: Polity.

Frey, R. G. 1977. Animal Rights. *Analysis* 37(4): 186–189.

Fricker, M. 2007. *Epistemic Injustice: Power and the Ethics and Knowing.* Oxford: Oxford University Press.

Fried, Charles. 1978. *Right and Wrong.* Cambridge, MA: Harvard University Press.

Geffen, Nathan. 2009. Justice after AIDS denialism: should there be prosecutions and compensation? *Journal of Acquired Immune Deficiency Syndrome* 51(4): 454–455.

Gewirth, Alan. 1981. Are There Any Absolute Rights? *The Philosophical Quarterly* 31(122): 1–16.

Ginet, Carl. 2001. Deciding to Believe. In: Steup, Matthias (ed.) *Knowledge, Truth, and Duty*. Oxford: Oxford University Press, 63–76.

Ginsborg, Hannah. 2007. Reasons for belief. *Philosophy and Phenomenological Research* 72: 286–318.

Glendon, Mary Ann. 1991. *Rights Talk: The Impoverishment of Political Discourse*. New York: The Free Press.

Goldberg-Hiller, Jonathan and Milner, Neal. 2003. Rights as Excess: Understanding the Politics of Special Rights. *Law and Social Inquiry* 28(4): 1075–1118.

Graham, Paul. 1996. The Will Theory of Rights: A Defence. *Law and Philosophy* 15(3): 257–270.

Grebe, Eduard and Nattrass, Nicoli. 2011. AIDS Conspiracy Beliefs and Unsafe Sex in Cape Town. *AIDS and Behavior* 16: 761–773.

Haack, Susan. 1997. 'The Ethics of Belief' Reconsidered. In: Hahn, Lewis Edwin (ed.) *The Philosophy of Roderick M. Chisholm, vol xxv of The Library of Living Philosophers*. Chicago: Open Court.

Hall, Richard and Johnson, Charles. 1998. The Epistemic Duty to Seek More Evidence. *American Philosophical Quarterly* 35(2): 129–139.

Harding, Sandra. 1986. *The Science Question in Feminism*. Ithaca: Cornell University Press.

Hart, H. L. A. 1982. *Essays on Bentham: Jurisprudence and Political Philosophy*. Oxford: Oxford University Press.

Hart, H. L. A. 1955. Are there any natural rights? *The Philosophical Review* 64 (2): 175–191.

Hartney, Michael. 1991. Some Confusions Concerning Collective Rights. *Canadian Journal of Law & Jurisprudence* 4(2): 293–314.

Hill Collins, Patricia. 1986. Learning from the Outsider Within: The Sociological Significance and Black Feminist Thought. *Social Problems* 33(6): 14–32.

Hill Collins, Patricia. 2000. *Black Feminist Thought: Knowledge, Consciousness and the Politics of Empowerment*. New York: Routledge.

Hohfeld, Wesley Newcombe, 1919. *Fundamental Legal Conceptions as Applied in Judicial Reasoning*, W.W. Cooke (ed.), New Haven: Yale University Press.

Institute of Medicine and the National Academy of Sciences. *Confronting AIDS: Update 1988*. Washington D.C.: National Academy Press.

Jae Joon Chung and Junxia Liu. 2018. The abolition of the adultery law in South Korea: A critique. *Asian Journal of Women's Studies* 24(2): 205–223.

Jaggar, Alison, M. 1983. *Feminist Politics and Human Nature*. Oxford: Rowman & Littlefield.

Jaggar, Alison, M. 1989. Love and Knowledge: Emotion in Feminist Epistemology in (eds.) Jaggar, Alison M. and Bordo, Susan R. *Gender/Body/Knowledge: Feminist Reconstructions of Being and Knowing*, New Brunswick: Rutgers University Press, pp. 145–171.

James, William. 1896 [1956]. *The Will to Believe and other essays in popular philosophy*. New York: Dover Publications, pp. 1–31.

Jones, Vivien (ed.). 2006. *Women in the Eighteenth Century: Constructions of Femininity*. London: Routledge.

Kalichman, Seth. C. 2009. *Denying AIDS: conspiracy theories, pseudoscience, and human tragedy*. New York and London: Copernicus/Springer.

Kalichman, Seth C. 2014. The Psychology of AIDS Denialism: Pseudoscience, Conspiracy Thinking, and Medical Mistrust. *European Psychologist* 19: 13–22.

Kamm, Frances. 2007. *Intricate Ethics*. Oxford: Oxford University Press.

Kant, Immanuel. *The Metaphysics of Morals*. Cambridge: Cambridge University Press.

Kidd, Ian James and Carel, Havi. 2017. Epistemic Injustice and Illness. *Journal of Applied Philosophy* 34(2): 172–190.

Lackey, Jennifer (ed.). 2014. *Essays in Collective Epistemology*. Oxford: Oxford University Press.

Levy, Neil. 2007. Doxastic Responsibility. *Synthese* 155: 127–155.

Lomasky, Loren. 1987. *Persons, Rights, and the Moral Community*. Oxford: Oxford University Press.

Marmor, Andrei. 1997. On the limits of rights. *Law and Philosophy* 16: 1–18.

Marcosson, Samuel, A. 1995. The special rights canard in the debate over lesbian and gay civil rights. *Notre Dame Journal of Law, Ethics & Public Policy* 9(1): 137–184.

Mathieson, Kay. 2006. The Epistemic Features of Group Belief. *Episteme* 2(3): 161–175.

Medina, José. 2011. The Relevance of Credibility Excess in a Proportional View of Epistemic Injustice: Differential Epistemic Authority and the Social Imaginary. *Social Epistemology* 25(1): 15–35.

Medina, José. 2013. *The epistemology of resistance: Gender and racial oppression, epistemic injustice, and the social imagination*. Oxford: Oxford University Press.

Medina, José. 2021. Vices of the Privileged and Virtues of the Oppressed in Epistemic Group Dynamics in *The Routledge Handbook of Political Epistemology* edited by Michael Hannon and Jeroen de Ridder. London: Routledge.

Meier, Barry. 2018. *Pain Killer: An Empire Of Deceit And The Origin Of America's Opioid Epidemic*. New York: Random House.

Mill, John Stuart, 1969 [1861]. Utilitarianism in J. Robson (ed.), *The Collected Works of John Stuart Mill*, Vol 10, Toronto: Toronto University Press; London: Routledge & Kegan Paul, p. 203.

Mills, Charles. 1998. *Blackness Visible: Essays on Philosophy and Race*. Ithaca: Cornell University Press.

Milner, Neal. 1989. The Denigration of Rights and the Persistence of Rights Talk: A Cultural Portrait. *Law and Social Inquiry* 14(4): 631–675.

Montmarquet, James. 1992. Epistemic Virtue and Doxastic Responsibility. *American Philosophical Quarterly* 29(4): 331–341.

Moore, John. P. 2009. The dangers of denying HIV. *Nature* 459: 168.

Muga Wycliffe. 2009. When public negligence can become criminal. *African Business*, May.

Nagel, Thomas. 1986. *The View From Nowhere*. Oxford: Oxford University Press.

Nagel, Thomas. 1995. Personal Rights and Public Space. *Philosophy & Public Affairs* 24(2): 83–107.

Narveson, Jan. 1987. On a case for animal rights. *The Monist* 70(1): 31–49.

Nattrass, Nicoli. 2010. Still Crazy After All These Years: The Challenge of AIDS Denialism for Science. *AIDS and Behavior* 14: 248–251.

Nattrass, Nicoli and Kalichman, Seth C. 2009. The Politics and Psychology of AIDS Denialism in Poul Rohleder, Leslie Swartz, Seth C. Kalichman and Leickness C. Simbayi (eds.) *HIV/AIDS in South Africa 25 Years On*. New York: Springer.

O'Brien, Stephen J. and Goedert, James J. 1996. HIV causes AIDS: Koch's postulates fulfilled. *Current Opinion in Immunology* 8(5): 613–618.

O'Neill, Onora. 1988. Children's rights and children's lives. *Ethics* 98: 445–463.

O'Neill, Onora. 2005. The dark side of human rights. *International Affairs* 81(2): 427–439.

Partridge, Ernest. 1981. Posthumous Interests and Posthumous Respect. *Ethics* 91: 243–64.

Pieterse, Marius. 2007. Eating Socioeconomic Rights: The Usefulness of Rights Talk in Alleviating Social Hardship Revisited. *Human Rights Quarterly* 29(3): 796–822.

Proctor, Roert. N. 2011. *Golden Holocaust: Origins of the Cigarette Catastrophe and the Case for Abolition*. Berkeley: University of California Press.

Purdue Pharma. 1996. New hope for millions of Americans suffering from persistent pain. Press release. Available at: http://www.documentcloud.org/documents/2815975-Pressreleaseversionone.html

Raible, Lea. 2020. *Human Rights Unbound: A Theory of Extraterritoriality*. Oxford: Oxford University Press.

Rainbolt, George. 2006. Rights Theory. *Philosophy Compass* 1(1): 11–21.

Raz, Joseph. 1984. On the nature of rights. *Mind* 93(370): 194-214.

Regan, Tom. 1992. The Case for Animal Rights. In: Jeffrey Olen and Vincent Barry (eds.) *Applying Ethics*. Belmont, CA: Wadsworth Publishing Co.

Richardson, Brian. 2004. The Public's Right to Know: A Dangerous Notion. *Journal of Mass Media Ethics* 19(1): 46–55.

Robert, C., Gallo, M. D. and Luc Montagnier, M. D. 2003. The discovery of HIV as the cause of AIDS. *New England Journal of Medicine* 349: 2283–2285.

Robertson, John, A. 2011. Abortion and technology: Sonograms, fetal pain, viability, and early prenatal diagnosis. *University of Pennsylvania Journal of Constitutional Law*, 14(2): 327–390.

Rowlands, S. 2011. Misinformation on abortion. *The European Journal of Contraception & Reproductive Health Care* 16(4): 233–240.

Russell, Bruce. 2001. Epistemic and Moral Duty. In: Steup, Matthias (ed.) *Knowledge, Truth, and Duty*. Oxford: Oxford University Press, pp. 34–48.

Smith, Rhona, K. M. 2020. *International Human Rights Law*. Oxford: Oxford University Press.

Singer, Peter. 1995. *Animal Liberation*. London: Pimlico.

Sreenivasan, Gopal. 2005. A Hybrid Theory of Claim-Rights. *Oxford Journal of Legal Studies* 25(2): 257–274.

Sreenivasan, Gopal. 2010. Duties and Their Direction. *Ethics* 120(3): 465–494.

Steup, Matthias. 2001. Epistemic Duty, Evidence, and Internality. In: Steup, Matthias (ed.) *Knowledge, Truth, and Duty*. Oxford: Oxford University Press, pp. 134–150.

Thomson, Judith Jarvis, 1990. *The Realm of Rights*. Cambridge, MA: Harvard University Press.

Van Zee, Art. 2009. The promotion and marketing of oxycontin: commercial triumph, public health tragedy. *American Journal of Public Health* 99(2): 221–227.

Vosoughi, Soroush, Roy, Deb and Aral, Sinan. 2018. The spread of true and false news online. *Science* 359(6380): 1146–1151.

Wainberg, Mark. 2004. In: Scovill, R. *The other side of AIDS* (film). Available at: http://www.theothersideofaids.com/free_to_ question.html.

Watson, Lani. 2018a. Curiosity and Inquisitiveness. In *The Routledge Handbook of Virtue Epistemology* edited by Heather Battaly. New York: Routledge.

Watson, Lani. 2018b. Systematic Epistemic Rights Violations in the Media: A Brexit Case Study. *Social Epistemology*, 32(2): 88–102.

Watson, Lani. 2020. Epistemic Rights in a Polarised World: The Right to Know and the Abortion Debate. In: Tanesini, Alessandra and Lynch, Michael (eds.) *Polarisation, Arrogance, and Dogmatism: Philosophical Perspectives*. London: Routledge.

Weller, Kondwani, Webber, Sheila and Levy, Philippa. 2017. Myths about HIV and AIDS among serodiscordant couples in Malawi. *Aslib Journal of Information Management* 69(3): 278–293.

Wellman, Carl. 1995. *Real Rights*. New York: Oxford University Press.

Wenar, Leif. 2003. Epistemic Rights and Legal Rights. *Analysis* 63(278): 142–146.

Wenar, Leif. 2005. The Nature of Rights. *Philosophy & Public Affairs* 33(3): 223–252.

Wenar, Leif. 2013. The Nature of Claim-Rights. *Ethics* 123(2): 202–229.

Wenar, Leif. 2015. "Rights." *The Stanford Encyclopedia of Philosophy*, Edward N. Zalta (ed.). Accessed online: https://plato.stanford.edu/archives/fall2015/entries/rights/.

Wollstonecraft, Mary. 2004 [1792]. *A Vindication of the Rights of Woman*. London: Penguin Books.

Zagzebski, Linda. 1996. *Virtues of the Mind*. Oxford: Oxford University Press.

Index

Printed in the United States
by Baker & Taylor Publisher Services